GW00724762

THE INVESTED INVESTOR

THE NEW RULES FOR START-UPS, SCALE-UPS AND ANGEL INVESTING

Published by Invested Investor Limited

© Invested Investor Limited and Peter Cowley 2018

Edition one, 2018
This is edition two, 2019

www.investedinvestor.com

Peter Cowley has asserted his right under the Copyright, Designs and Patents Act, 1988, to be identified as the author of this work

All rights reserved. No part of this publication may be reproduced, stored in a retrieval system, or transmitted, in any form, or by any means, electronic, mechanical, photocopying, recording or otherwise, without prior permission, in writing, from the publisher.

Text and cover designed by Paul Parrett Book Production, www.pbbp.co.uk
Illustrations by Neil Kerber
Project management: Sally Simmons (s.simmons@camedit.com)
and Rosalind Horton (r.horton@camedit.com)

ISBN
978-1-9164079-2-3 (hard cover)
978-1-9164079-0-9 (paperback)
978-1-9164079-1-6 (ebook)

Citations

This remarkable book traces Peter Cowley's personal journey from being an entrepreneur and a business angel to an Invested Investor. It also interweaves decades of his own "lessons learned" with those of other entrepreneurs and angel investors, so that it simultaneously constitutes a major piece of research, all the while having the slight flavour of being a mystery story. You cannot wait until you get to the end to find out how it all worked out! The readers, be they angel investors, entrepreneurs, or even policy makers, researchers, and large corporations seeking to find the secrets of innovation and scaling up, will be well rewarded with this insightful, eminently useful and readable book. It is well worth the time invested to read and to keep on coming back to as a reference over and over again.

Candace Johnson – Serial Entrepreneur and Angel Investor, SES Astra, SES Global, Loral Teleport Europe, Europe Online, EBAN President Emeritus, OWNSAT-Kacific

Peter's candid and transparent approach is a what the start-up world needs. This book helps both investors and entrepreneurs understand the mind of an invested investor.

Jon Bradford – Founding Partner, Motive Partners and the Godfather of European Accelerators

Peter is a unique angel investor in that he is absolutely tireless at passing on his hard-won knowledge of starting deep tech businesses and making them successful. He works extremely hard with aspiring entrepreneurs and helps them to beat the odds every step of the way through a combination of great knowledge and forthright coaching. When I first heard him use the expression 'The Invested Investor', I immediately understood the concept and have been using the expression myself and extolling its virtues. I am

delighted that Peter is formalising this approach and turning it into a model for business angels and investors. Successful start-up investment is so much more than the financial transaction and this method will help to keep Angel investing rich, enjoyable and successful.
Robert Marshall – CEO, Marshall Group

I have made my way through the chapters with great interest and finding the book both informative and a real pleasure to read. No mean feat! I was particularly struck by your comments at the top of page 66!
Catherine Lewis La Torre – CEO, British Business Investments & British Patient Capital

Combining humor and deep insights, Peter Cowley delves into the opportunities and obstacles of being a successful angel investor. Whether, you are a new angel, a seasoned angel, or just someone who wants to support innovative ideas, I highly recommend this book. It will likely save you a lot of mistakes and may even help you find some winners.
Linda Smith – Chair Emeritus, Angel Capital Association

Peter's honest approach gives entrepreneurs the chance to understand the mindset of the investor & that not all investors are equal.
Hanadi Jabado – Director of Enterprise, Cambridge Judge Business School

What I liked about this book was how candid the author was on investing returns – in that one should expect lots of failures along with the few successes – if one has made enough investments. He also has a good set of case studies of real-life companies with surprising amount of inside detail which is normally hidden. This book is great for first time and seasoned angel investors. Although it has a UK emphasis, the lessons are good for investors in any country.

**Ronjon Nag – Exited Entrepreneur,
Invested Investor and Stanford Distinguished
Careers Institute Interdisciplinary Fellow**

Advice may not always go to plan, but the advice Peter gives in this book is hugely useful to entrepreneurs looking for angel investment. His frank personality has produced a very readable and interesting insight on angel investing.

**Shirin Dehghan – Founder & CEO,
Arieso and Senior Partner, Frog Capital.**

I was preparing some classes for Cambridge Judge Business School for their Masters in Entrepreneurship and not surprisingly one of the reading materials will be the book by Peter Cowley. Great insight to Business Angel thoughts.

Goncalo de Vasconcelos – Founder & CEO, SyndicateRoom

Straight-forward, wise and practical advice from the Archangel of Angels. Well worth reading for entrepreneurs, angels and advisors.

Martin Frost – Founder & CEO, CMR Surgical

It reads well and has good cartoons. A useful reminder to those of us in the industry of what we should be doing, a guide for new angels; but in my opinion particularly good for entrepreneurs to help them understand how private investors think.

**Struan McDougall – Founder & Chairman,
Cambridge Capital Group**

The candid, honest, war story approach resonates with the way I like to help start-ups.

**Ian Tracey – Head of Access to Funding & Finance
at The Knowledge Transfer Network (KTN)**

The Invested Investor book provides an excellent insight into the way angel investors think.

Mark Littlewood – CEO, Business of Software Conference

This book is dedicated to two people who died too young: my close friend and angel mentor, Nat Billington and my son, Ian/Nam, who wrote the verse below to help me overcome my fear of public speaking. He succeeded, giving me the confidence to travel the world sharing my experiences of angel investing with thousands of people.

Nervousness to a crowd

Feel that heart start to pound, before you even stand
Somewhere in your body, that sped-up beat is being
    highlighted
A look around in front of you confirms, that yes, you are
    standing with hundreds of eyes on you
You find it hard to move, as your now rigid body tightens
The words come thin and fast, though they can't find that
    dancing enthusiasm now
Relax
Breathe in… breathe out… aaaarrr
Free the tension that holds you, let it go
These beings that are watching and listening, make no
    judgements
They and you are we
We have all come to be in joy
To share and experience each other's creativity
So relax my friend, hang loose
For that nervousness has been replaced, that fear has been
    replaced
With confidence… With love
Relax and embrace this moment to share…

A note to investors and entrepreneurs around the world

This book is packed with universal principles for investors and entrepreneurs wherever they are – but it won't take you long to work out that I'm British. Any references to tax and other legal requirements relating to investing are the situation in the UK, at the time of writing. If you are investing outside the UK, naturally you'll check what applies in your judiciary, won't you?

Disclaimer

Angel investing carries very high risks and should not be under-taken lightly. I am sharing multiple experiences and lessons I have learned from several decades of building companies and investing in start-ups, but please be aware that you must make your own decisions about whether angel investing is right for you and, if so, how you will go about it. Do not invest money that you cannot afford to lose in start-up businesses.

Acknowledgements

Thanks first, to my kids (Matt, Ian and Alan) who, being millennials taught me so much (how else does a baby boomer learn to avoid FOMO?), especially Alan, who as my cofounder of the Invested Investor (my 12th start-up, his first) copes with my crazy ideas and tight deadlines. To my wife, Alison, who allows me to be over-busy, yet find time to have holidays and a social life.

Next to Katy Tuncer, who, four years ago, became a mentee, my business life coach and a friend, which started with asking for my help with her start-up (now classed as an elegant failure) and very soon telling me that I needed to learn to say 'no', with which I still struggle.

And Kate Kirk (who will always be able to wordsmith and play better real tennis than me), Jonno Brech (our marketing guru who challenges any assumption) and Brian Harris (who chose the name and helped define the tone).

To my focus groups who gave me a regular and well-deserved battering. Entrepreneurs: David Buxton, James Hyde and James Strachan, William Makant and Yusuf Muhammad, Alex Schey and Toby Schulz, Raph Scheps and Gideon Farrell. Angels: Simon Thorpe, Rajat Malhotra and Tim Parsonson. And Suezann Holmes who has been CFO of four of my boards.

To the team we have built to create podcasts, write the book and spread the word: Kate Kirk, Soraya Jones, Mark Cotton, Neil Kerber, Ingrid Sims, Simon Hall, Phil Sansom, Sally Simmons, Paul Barrett and Ros Horton.

The book was critiqued (sometimes quite severely) in a short time by a great group of reviewers: Inger Anson, Paul Anson, Ludo Chapman, Brian Harris, Suezann Holmes, Sheila Kissane-Marshall, Peter Last, Alison Lloyd, Richard Lucas, Ron Metcalfe,

Emmi Nicholl, Robert Sansom, James Strachan, Simon Thorpe, Katy Tuncer, Mac Tuncer and Mike Walker.

Much of the content has come from interviewing the 50-plus people, who have been open and honest about their journeys and advice, for our podcasts, articles and videos.

To friends: Martin Kleppmann, who took my first angel investment in 2007, Chris Smith, owner of the Naked Scientists programme, who taught me how to interview, Nat Billington, from whom I learned so much, and Robert Marshall and Tim Mills, who had faith in my abilities before I knew I had them.

To the very many people who assisted me in my metamorphosis from a keen but not very successful entrepreneur to a keen and, hopefully, more successful angel investor. I can't name you all, but you know who you are.

And of course to the Cambridge Angels (founded by Robert Sansom and David Cleevely), who taught me everything I know about angel investing.

I have often described this as a 'readable reference book', and to allow you to search the text you have access to the whole book in electronic form, on our investedinvestor.com website using the **codeword: investedinvestor18**. We will add further content for those who have read this, including early access to the next book.

Contents

CHAPTER 1

Why I'm an invested investor

My name is Peter and I am an invested investor. I'm a Yorkshireman, an entrepreneur and a business angel who firmly believes that founders of start-up companies should get far more than just money from their investors.

I also believe that entrepreneurs need to know how their investors think, what their motives are and how to get the best out of them, because starting and growing a company is a long-term project and the investor-investee relationship is crucial. So while this book is directed primarily at investors, I'm hoping that those on the other side of the table, the entrepreneurs and founders, will also benefit from what I and others have to say.

Like any marriage, the investor/investee relationship will need work from time to time. Hence this warts-and-all guide to how to be an angel, built from my own personal experiences and those of the many hundreds of brilliant investors and founders I have spoken to and worked with over the years.

> ❧ There's nothing quite like seeing a company you've nurtured and supported from birth reach a successful exit.

My journey to becoming an invested investor
I stumbled into angel investing over ten years ago.

Having founded and run more than ten start-ups since the early 1980s, I decided it was time to give something back. I set up an alumni mentoring scheme with my old department at the University of Cambridge and went along to one of their meetings. There I met a young computer science graduate called Martin Kleppmann. Martin had come back to Cambridge to set up a company but had no idea what that company might do or how to go about setting it up. I joined him on his first journey into entrepreneurship, learning a lot myself along the way.

Martin had lots of crazy ideas and deep technical expertise but didn't know how to identify a business opportunity based on that expertise, nor how he should go about finding what he could sell to customers. He had one idea that sounded promising, so I suggested he do some market research. In what I later found was typical Martin fashion, he gathered a huge amount of data – but the data showed that his idea was too difficult technically and that people wouldn't pay for it anyway.

Nevertheless, he was determined to start a company and had faith that he would come up with the right product. He started out by consulting and doing contract work as a web developer, often a good way to find out where the pain points are in a system, while putting a bit of money aside to fund product development in the future. This was in the days before the browser system consolidated into just the few we use today and it was a time-consuming and laborious process making JavaScript work across the different browsers. Martin knew he could come up with an automated system to solve this problem. The difficulty was in getting people to incorporate it into their workflow as, despite its being lauded as a great idea, nobody wanted to invest the time and effort into learning how to use it.

Through a stroke of serendipity, Martin and his small team moved into the premises of another company, Redgate Software, and this eventually led to an exit less than three years later. During this time, I learned the meaning of the word 'angel' in the context of early stage investing, how much I enjoyed helping young entrepreneurs and how much more I had to learn.

The next stage in my angel investing journey was to join a group of investors known as the Cambridge Angels. New members have to be sponsored by an existing member and I was lucky enough to be introduced to the group by one of the founders, Robert Sansom. With plenty of help and advice from the other members of the group, I began investing actively in start-ups. I knew I'd experienced most of the good and bad times a company can go through and started building a network of investors and entrepreneurs. I felt that I could not only make a return but also, and more importantly, help start-up companies to avoid some of the pitfalls I'd become so familiar with on my own entrepreneurial journeys.

Since then, I've invested in more than 65 early stage companies. I've had over 8,000 business plans arrive in my Inbox, seen 1,000 live pitches, sat on a dozen start-up boards and mentored hundreds of entrepreneurs. I've held meetings on the London Tube and mentoring sessions while walking in the Welsh mountains, and heard countless war stories from my fellow angels and entrepreneurs.

At a rough estimate, I've spent 50,000 hours as an entrepreneur and 15,000 as an angel, helping and advising start-ups and scale-ups. Malcolm Gladwell and others claim that mastering a skill is said to require 10,000 hours of training and experience, so I ought to know what I'm doing by now – but I'm still learning.

Experience doesn't necessarily lead to success. Even with my many years in entrepreneurship and investing, and with all the lessons I've learned along the way, I know that being an angel is not an easy way to get rich. Or even comfortable. I'll be blunt, it's bloody difficult just to break even. Angel investing is as hard as entrepreneurship itself; it's demanding, arduous and often disheartening, and like all angel investors I see failures more often than glorious exits (although angels hope that the exits will more than compensate for the losses).

Nevertheless, I'm writing a book about how to be a better business angel, what I call an invested investor. Yes, there are risks and yes, it's hard work, but the rewards are more than financial. It's fun, even when it's tough, and there's nothing quite like seeing a company you've nurtured from birth reach a successful exit.

From angels to invested investors

Business angels can and should be a powerful force for growing our economy. The world needs bright, ambitious entrepreneurs with brilliant ideas who will develop the products, services and technologies of the future, but it also needs business angels to provide the investment those entrepreneurs need to get their ideas off the ground.

The UK Business Angels Association, UKBAA (a not-for-profit trade body, of which I am a non-executive director), estimates that there are around 18,000 business angels in the UK who invest over £1.3 billion in start-ups and early stage businesses each year. InvestEurope reported €649 million in seed funding and €3.5 billion in start-up investment across Europe in 2017. In the US, estimates from the Angel Capital Association indicate that there are around 300,000 business angels who collectively invested over $25 billion in 2017.

But survival rates for new companies are poor. Various sources claim that around 50% of new businesses don't last longer than five years and only a third make it to their tenth anniversary. Some state that as many as 90% of new businesses fail.

Why are so many start-ups failing? The 2015–16 Global Entrepreneurship Monitor Report claimed that around half of business failures are due to lack of profit or lack of funding. But why don't they make a profit? And why can't they secure further funding to help them on the path to profitability or exit?

I'd argue that one of the reasons for these high failure rates is because entrepreneurs need more than money if they are going to build successful companies and change the world. What they need are not just angels in the traditional sense, but also angels who are what I have termed invested investors.

What is an invested investor? Invested investors not only provide money, but also help entrepreneurs as they build their business. They have money that they're willing to risk losing, experience in the sector their entrepreneurs are targeting and contacts that can help the new business find customers, suppliers and management skills. They also recognise when to re-invest, when to look for investors with bigger pockets, and when to fold.

What are the attributes of an invested investor?

They're comfortable with risk.

They have money they're willing to lose.

They are willing to work hard to help entrepreneurs launch and grow their ventures.

They have experience and contacts that are useful to the entrepreneurs they support.

They recognise that it will almost certainly take more than one round of funding to grow a company.

They know that companies often fail.

They never regret the big one that got away.

They act in an open and transparent way with founders and fellow investors.

They are emotionally intelligent and can see things from the entrepreneurs' point of view, even when they don't agree with them.

They don't blame others when an investment is lost.

They see good exits as providing more money for them to invest in start-ups.

They never stop learning.

Business angels are not saintly figures handing out money to every entrepreneur they meet. They are early stage investors who put thousands of pounds and more of their own money into fledgling businesses. They want to make a return on their money, and they want to find and invest in the entrepreneurs who will give them that return by building a successful business. But they also know that they're taking a risk and that they're investing money that they may never see again.

Being an angel is not about spotting 'the one', although we've all heard of the people who made millions, billions even, buying

a few shares in Amazon or Google when they started out. Andy Bechtolsheim, co-founder of Sun Microsystems, was born on the same day as me; we both studied computer science at university, we're both entrepreneurs and we've both lived in Bavaria. He's a highly successful serial entrepreneur and what I'd call a very invested investor. I rang him a few days before our sixtieth birthdays to compare notes. One noticeable difference between us was that Andy made a $100k investment in Google pre-incorporation, which, if he hasn't sold, will now be worth $3.5 billion.

But we've also all heard about the dozen or more publishers who turned down the first Harry Potter book, missing out on the billions to be made from the boy wizard. And if you're a *Dragons' Den* or *Shark Tank* fan, how many of the companies that pitched successfully have become household names? For every success story, there are many failures, and for every lucky or inspired pick, there are plenty of also-rans. There are no guarantees that the companies you invest in, however much work you do before – and after – signing on the dotted line, will take the market by storm. Unicorns were mythical creatures long before the world of venture capital (VC) appropriated the term for that almost-as-rare animal, the privately owned start-up valued at $1billion or more.

Writing a cheque and sitting back waiting for a bigger cheque in return may technically make you an angel but not the sort of angel I'm interested in developing. Yes, there are plenty of angels who do just that, put in their money and wait– perhaps they even remember to keep their fingers crossed. There are also many angels who only make one or two investments. Perhaps they don't have the cash or the appetite to support more start-ups, or perhaps they see their first investments fail and are put off taking any more risks.

There is nothing intrinsically wrong with having passive investors in the ecosystem; after all, entrepreneurs do need money to employ great people and build their businesses. But experience has taught me that invested investors have a greater chance of success. They won't necessarily be closely engaged with all of their investments on a regular basis, they probably won't have the time, but they will be as active as they can be and ready to help when needed.

Invested investors know that angel investing is hard work and if they are going to make a return – possibly one that helps them invest in even more start-ups – then they have to be willing to put in the effort. My friend Simon Thorpe, for instance, is a very invested investor. He keeps an extensive record of the 30 or so companies in his portfolio and checks regularly to see what's going on. He reviews each company and asks himself, 'Have I spoken to them recently? What value can I add at this stage in their journey? What have I noticed in the sector that might be useful to them? Who do I know who could help them?' For companies where he's on the

Board, he'll attend 6–12 meetings each year and put in more time if the company is going through a particularly difficult or exciting phase and needs his help.

Most invested investors never really retire. I may make fewer new investments and focus more closely on the companies already in my portfolio as I look at what I want to do in the next phase of my life, but I know I'll never really wind down completely. There are still plenty of good ideas out there and in writing this book, I'm hoping to continue to benefit angels and entrepreneurs long after I've stopped being such an active angel myself. So I, along with one of my sons and a group of like-minded contributors, have launched the Invested Investor project. It's a big risk for me, as it's business to consumer (B2C), whereas I'm most comfortable with business to business (B2B), and involves publishing and audience building, areas where I have no experience. But entrepreneurs are natural risk-takers and that urge never goes away.

The importance of transparency

> Invested investors work with their entrepreneurs in an open and transparent way, so that secrets never get in the way of progress – they act as mentor, collaborator and even friend. They know that transparency in the relationship always works, even when it feels inappropriate or difficult.

In this book, I hope to do two things. I want to teach you how to become an invested investor and help to grow better companies, and I also want to demonstrate the importance of trust and transparency in creating the type of mutually beneficial relationships that will help those companies flourish.

First, I want to take you through the many aspects of angel investing and point out the potential pitfalls so you can avoid them. Just as the lifecycle of a company is not a straight line from the initial idea to success (or failure), the investment cycle for an angel is full of twists and turns. You need to know what to expect, and when your entrepreneurs are going to need extra help to overcome the inevitable challenges they will face.

I believe that many people who could be angels are put off by a lack of confidence, feeling that they don't understand exactly what is involved, or simply don't know where to start. By describing the investment journey and the hazards along the way, I hope to dispel their fears and make the first step that much easier to take. There's no reason why you should make the same mistakes that I made. If you can take a few shortcuts based on my advice, then do it.

Second, by being honest about the ups and downs of my own investing life, and describing the adventures of other experienced angels and entrepreneurs, I hope to show how important it is to build open and trusting relationships with both your entrepreneurs and your fellow investors. Secrets and misconceptions can be seriously damaging in any relationship and the business relationship is no exception.

> Angels need to spot good business opportunities and entrepreneurs need to find angels who will help them build a successful business – but without honesty and trust, neither of these things can happen.

Is this book for you?
In this book, I will tell you about all the things I and others have done wrong. I will share the many things I wish someone had told me ten years ago about being an early stage investor. I will explain the model I've devised based on every disaster and screw-up I've suffered. And I'll show you how I use my model to assess and manage investment opportunities rationally and, at times, ruthlessly.

I'm writing this book primarily for other angels, or those who are considering putting on their wings for the first time. But I believe that much of what I've come to know is of value to entrepreneurs as well. Entrepreneurs who can see the world through the eyes of their investors and understand their behaviours and motivations are much more likely to build the foundations on which to succeed.

Each chapter ends with a story, from an entrepreneur or from an investor, highlighting the many challenges that they've faced at one time or another. You can hear the subjects of those stories talking about their experiences in greater detail on the Invested Investor website, www.investedinvestor.com. The website also has a wealth of additional material, including more of the many interviews I and my son, Alan, carried out for the Invested Investor project. I've also included a glossary covering the multitude of terms that are the jargon of angel investing, and a list of websites for the organisations mentioned to help you find out more about them and what they have to offer.

In the end, the only way to become a successful angel investor is to take the plunge and write that first cheque, knowing that there's probably a long journey (and more cheques) ahead. I'm going to share my experiences and knowledge, but they are just that – mine – and shouldn't be taken as prescriptive or the be-all and end-all. Your experience, your sector knowledge and your risk profile will inevitably be different from mine. But hopefully, by the end of this book, you should be able to decide for yourself whether you have the energy, the time, the patience, the persistence and, yes, the money, to be an invested investor.

Read on if:
> You want to become an angel investor but don't know where to start.
> You want to learn what angel investing involves.
> You want to understand some of the potential pitfalls of angel investing and ways to avoid them – or at least lessen their impact.

> You want to help entrepreneurs build successful businesses.
> You are willing to risk your money and work hard, even though you know the chances of success are slim.

AN ENTREPRENEUR'S STORY:
My Camdata rollercoaster

Not all invested investors are former entrepreneurs, but plenty are, and they carry the battle scars to prove it. Here's my most dramatic entrepreneurial journey – one that isn't over yet.

In 1980, my fiancée and I moved to Germany where I was to join Ulbrich Automation. I had been working for Logica on a project to automate a new Whitbread brewery in South Wales, which included buying equipment from Ulbrich, and they had been trying to poach me for some time. Unfortunately, when I got to Germany, I found a company that was already struggling. It was suffering from 'creeping excellence', continually improving the product but not delivering to customers, and cash was always in short supply. Ulbrich's solution was to be acquired by Heckler and Koch, and I found myself potentially writing software for a weapons manufacturer.

That had not been my goal in going to Germany. Hence, a year after arriving, a colleague, Georg Pyttel, and I set up my first company, Gercom GmbH. We developed, manufactured and sold rugged computer equipment to industry, with me contributing the technical expertise and experience in international distribution and Georg providing management and product engineering. We were quite a family affair – Georg's wife was our office manager, Georg's father-in-law provided the capital and Georg's brother ran production.

The birth of my first son, Matt, meant time for a re-think. In 1984, we moved back to the UK and I founded a new company – Camdata Systems Ltd. The only funding Camdata Systems ever received came right at the start, from my parents and from a chartered accountant friend, Simon Mabey.

Camdata Systems started trading in 1984 as the UK agent for Gercom. There were already two resellers in the UK for Gercom, and Camdata Systems acted as a value-adding agent between Gercom and them. It wasn't very lucrative since the margins were small, so I also took some consultancy work as a programmer to make ends meet.

Many companies find themselves at the mercy of fluctuations in the wider world over which they have no control and Camdata Systems was no exception. In 1985, the pound fell sharply against the Deutsche Mark. Products from Germany suddenly became very expensive to UK customers and work with Gercom virtually disappeared. I decided Camdata Systems would develop its own products and one of the first contracts I secured was with Britoil, which was exploiting North Sea oil. I started hiring people and things were looking promising.

By the end of the 1980s, we had around 25 employees in two premises and 60–70 customers across the telecoms sector, food and drink, the City, and oil and gas. But high interest rates and deepening uncertainty had already set the UK on the path to recession and early 1990 saw the start of a year of pain, with a series of redundancies as we tried to keep the company going. On 14 February 1991, Camdata went into creditors voluntary liquidation (CVL) (administration was not an option at that time).

Coincidentally, Camdata Systems was headquartered in the then Prime Minister's constituency and I was contacted by a BBC reporter on the very day we went into CVL. The reporter was ringing round companies in the constituency taking the temperature of industry in the face of the recession. I ended up on the local BBC *Look East* news programme that night commenting that my company had gone into liquidation but that I would almost certainly be setting up another business in the future.

Some of the staff and equipment from Camdata Systems moved over to one of our first suppliers, Artronics, a company that had been very loyal to us. Meanwhile, I set up a new company in 1991 for my consulting work, Axon Consultants. I bought back some of the original intellectual property (including drawings and tooling) from the liquidators at auction. I was actually trying to bid up some of the lots to get more money for our creditors but that meant I also won some, including some I didn't want. Another friend, Gerry Tuffs, also bought some of the IP and lent it to me and Axon Consultants. Gerry was the founder of MicroTerminals Ltd, which designed and built the rugged MicroScribe terminals used in industrial applications.

I then set up Axxon Communications Limited as I grew the business from a one-man band. It wasn't long before I had a letter from lawyers at Exxon complaining that they had global rights to any word with two consecutive 'x's in the name but they didn't pursue it. Finally – at least for this stage – I launched a new Camdata, Camdata Ltd, in 1995 and wrapped Axon and Axxon into the new company.

By 1998, the second incarnation of Camdata seemed to be doing all right; we had a big project for Royal Ordnance and things could have been good. But we'd under-quoted on the project and the company was losing money as a result. I ended up selling Camdata Ltd to MicroTerminals Ltd, bringing Gerry Tuffs back into the story.

The next twist came when MicroTerminals was struggling and I bought Camdata Ltd back from Gerry. He was an extremely good negotiator and I ended up paying a higher price to get my company back than he had paid for it six months beforehand.

In 2002, Gerry decided to shut down MicroTerminals. He already had other interests and the company had been in the doldrums for a while. So I bought MicroTerminals and resurrected some Microscribe products, secured projects with Domino Printing, among many others, and the company lives on today. My return on investment in MicroTerminals was more than 50x and Gerry went on to build and sell the largest free-range egg business in Wales.

Today, Camdata still sells the MicroScribe and is the sole distributor in the UK for a piece of maintenance equipment for the traffic light industry, a MicroTerminals legacy. It's really a lifestyle business now but worth keeping going, and is run by my younger son, Alan. I even switch on the soldering iron and oscilloscope occasionally and do some of the hands-on repair work myself, which has its own rewards.

So Camdata launched, suffered at the hands of the late 1980s' recession, failed, re-started, got sold, got bought, bought its previous acquirer, then bought our main competitor and is now profitable as a small lifestyle business. Did I learn any lessons? You bet, and I'll talk about them in the next chapter. In the meantime, when you see an engineer fixing a set of traffic lights, remember there are decades of drama in the equipment he's using!

CHAPTER 2

Are you ready to put on your wings?

efore I explain the different elements and stages of angel investing in more detail, we need to look at the basics. Do you know enough about the first principles of angel investing to be sure that you're ready and willing to don your wings and take off? In this chapter, I'm going to look at what you need to know in order to decide whether angel investing is for you. I'll discuss the fundamental importance of understanding your own risk profile and why you need to build a portfolio rather than putting all your eggs in one basket. I'll also look at what you might bring to the start-ups you get involved with, and the time you should expect to put in.

6 Taking off is optional, landing is mandatory.

Being an invested investor is not easy

The first time you do anything new is hard; adding a financial risk makes it even harder.

A lot of people start out by investing in a company being set up by someone they know. This categorises them as one of what are known affectionately as the three Fs – Family, Friends and Fools – and often gives the impression that making the first investment is easy. But investing in someone you already know, whether because you are related to them or like them, is fraught with its own difficulties. You may think they have a great idea but do you know much about their business and strategic capabilities?

Investing in a stranger is another thing entirely – even finding them in the first place is difficult. You can't build the kind of trusting and mutually supportive relationship overnight that is essential to success, but you won't have a lifetime to get to know them before you have to make the decision and stump up the cash.

You will be taking a leap into the unknown and if you think that is easy, you're probably not doing your due diligence thoroughly enough or you're making dangerous assumptions. Or perhaps you have so much money that you don't really care if you lose some, but I think that's unlikely.

Alternatively, you might think the first investment is easy because you've bought into a new company via a crowdfunding platform and have decided that makes you an angel. New angels are often advised to begin with crowdfunding, and I agree it's a good way to get started, but putting £50 into a company through crowdfunding most certainly does not make you an invested investor.

With crowdfunding, you might be able to build your portfolio quickly and easily from your front room but do you know what you're really getting for your money? Your only contact with the entrepreneurs will probably be the videos and pitch decks they upload to the platform and you're unlikely to be able to have a face-to-face conversation with them. Nor are you likely to be able to interact with any of the other investors in a meaningful way, although you may be able to learn a certain amount from their questions if there's a forum or chat room on the site.

Crowdfunded investments will be for small portions of the company; there will be many shareholders and you will have little or no opportunity to get to know the entrepreneurs properly and bring your experience into play – nor, indeed, offer them much advice if it's a sector you're familiar with.

I have to declare an interest here because I was an early investor in the equity investment platform Syndicate Room. The model for Syndicate Room is different from most other crowdfunding platforms because opportunities are introduced and led by experienced investors. This could provide the new angel with a better opportunity to learn the ins and outs of investing, but Syndicate Room is targeted at sophisticated investors who understand the risks and generally invest larger sums than the other platforms.

The bottom line is that no considered investment decision is easy.

> 'If you're going into angel investing then start slowly, because I'm going to promise you, you are not as good as you think you are.'
>
> Andy Phillipps, entrepreneur and investor

Have you got useful experience?

There are many ways in which your career or entrepreneurial experience can be useful to a start-up company. Valuable insights could come from your knowledge of a sector you've worked in for a substantial part of your career, your professional skills as a lawyer or accountant, or from the adventure of having been an entrepreneur yourself.

If you've had a career in the travel sector, common sense should tell you that making your first investment in telecoms is a mistake. What value can you add in a sector you know nothing about? But it's possible that your career in the travel sector was all about sales, and you may be able to transfer that knowledge to a different area, as long as you're careful not to fall into the one-size-fits-all trap and assume that all sales are made in exactly the same way.

If you've had a career as a lawyer or accountant, you can help first-time entrepreneurs recognise which professional services they must buy in and shouldn't attempt to tackle for themselves. Starting out with the correct structure and professional advice could well pay off later, when the company is bigger and things are more complicated.

Experience of starting and running a company yourself can help you to empathise with your investee companies. You may well be able to spot potential problems while they're still on the horizon and not staring the entrepreneurs in the face, and mitigate any negative effects. But you may also think that having done it once, or twice, you know all the answers. Any serial entrepreneur will tell you that's a mistake.

Among the many lessons I learned over the 30-plus years of the Camdata story are several that I frequently bring to the table when advising entrepreneurs and helping the companies in my portfolio. Here are a few:

- Have a good negotiator in the team – I found this out the hard way when Gerry made me pay more for Camdata than he had paid when he bought it from me in the first place.
- Watch where the revenues are coming from – when Camdata failed the first time, it had getting on for 70 customers but 97% of total revenue was from sales of capital equipment, and only

3% from ongoing revenues, mostly servicing and post-warranty repairs. The company had no continuing revenue streams from its customers. When the recession hit and capital projects started to dry up, customers retrenched, and one of the first things they stopped doing was buying new equipment.

- Sometimes you have to fire people – a very good programmer, who worked at five times the rate of anyone else, dangerously threatened one of his colleagues one day and had to be fired instantly.

- Sometimes you have to retain people you're not sure you want – another programmer, who wasn't so good technically, was nevertheless excellent with customers, an important skill.

- Don't forget to learn – towards the demise of Camdata in 1991, I wrote a weekly report to myself summarising all the positives and negatives over the preceding week. I suppose if I'd known then what I know now, I might have seen the patterns and problems earlier, but at least I was always looking closely at what we were doing and trying to learn from our mistakes. Looking back at the last few months before Camdata went into CVL in February 1991, I can see how hard we tried to keep going. Between 26 October 1990 and 12 February 1991, I recorded 50 meetings with customers, lawyers, accountants, the bank and potential investors, looking for a way to keep our heads above water. As late as November 1990 we were still thinking that seeking additional investment and trading out was the way forward, rather than liquidation.

- Keep an eye on cash flow – orders won't pay salaries until invoiced and the cash is in the bank, and sometimes it was nip and tuck whether we would last from one month to the next, especially when customers were also in trouble. However, we paid December 1990 salaries early because we had new orders that hinted things might be on firmer footing and we didn't want the team to worry that they wouldn't be paid at Christmas.

- Threats of legal action focus the mind but make things even more difficult – creditors were circling even while we were doing everything we could to secure new business and keep existing customers on board. At one point, I wrote, 'Several more writs arrived. Two car phones cut off.' And later, 'Writs now number 16.'
- It's very hard to make your friends redundant – even more so when the redundancies are spread out over a long period.
- Your salary is not sacred – I cut my salary to zero in January 1990, a year before Camdata went into CVL. We survived the year on my wife's salary and by making some changes to our lifestyle, but it wasn't easy.

All these lessons are as relevant to investing as they are to starting and growing a business.

Do you understand your own risk profile?

What are the risks involved in angel investing? The most obvious is that you will lose your money. So before you make an investment, you need to understand if you are in a position to take that risk. You must ask yourself, 'Can I afford to lose this money? Will my lifestyle be affected if I never see a return?' If that feels too uncomfortable, then you're not ready to invest in start-ups.

The fundamental question here is, are you what is termed a high-net-worth (HNW) individual or sophisticated investor? Having the capital invested in a house is not the same as having readily available capital to invest in a start-up. Different jurisdictions have differing definitions of HNW. The UK's Financial Conduct Authority classifies as HNW an individual who has an annual income of £100,000 or more, or £250,000 in liquid assets, excluding their primary residence and pension funds. You may also need to take your current situation into account as part of this calculation, including your age and whether or not you have dependents to support. Investments should be diversified across different assets and it is generally recommended that angel investments should comprise around 10%–15% of a diversified portfolio.

If you are sure that you have money available to invest, on the understanding that you may lose it, there are more risks to consider. The founders you are investing in may well be new to entrepreneurship and so they will be learning as they grow the company. However quickly they learn, the company may fail because of market fluctuations, unforeseen events or because a competitor gets there first. You can do your best to help with advice and mentoring, but ultimately there is little you can do to mitigate the fundamental external risks of launching a business in a highly competitive world.

Then there is the matter of time. Angel investing is a long-term proposition and should not be viewed as a source of regular income. While some investors do structure their portfolios so that at least some of their investments provide dividends, I am personally against this because I believe the cash is better retained and used to grow the company. If the founders want more cash out and the company can afford it, they should be awarded a performance-based bonus. You will almost certainly see your shares in the company get diluted as other investors come in on later rounds, and preference shares or options kick in – that is, you will own a smaller percentage of the company, albeit hopefully worth more as the price of each share has increased. Are you willing to wait eight to ten years before you even know if a positive return is likely?

All these are part of your risk profile – and only you can assess how comfortable you are with the different risks involved and the varying levels of control you may have over mitigating those risks.

> 'The goal is not to fail fast. The goal is to succeed over the long run. They are not the same thing.'
>
> Marc Andreessen, entrepreneur and investor

The importance of building a portfolio

I've mentioned that the sum of all your investments should be diversified across a portfolio of different assets. Each asset will probably consist of a number of investments, a portfolio within a portfolio, and angel investing is no exception. Wise angels know that they have to build a portfolio – investing in high-risk start-ups is the perfect example of why you shouldn't put all your eggs in one basket. By investing in multiple companies, angels diversify, which mitigates the risks and also increases their chances of success.

How many companies should be in that portfolio? There are plenty of different theories as to why an angel investment portfolio should include a particular number of companies, indicating that it is far from an exact science.

One calculation puts the minimum number at 15 for a statistical chance of success. But we all know that statistics don't predict the real future, only a possible future – theoretically, all 15 of your companies could fail or your first two companies could have spectacular exits (and then you enter the dangerous territory of thinking you know what you're doing).

Others think 15 companies is too low but there are almost as many opinions as there are angels. David Rose, founder of the New York Angels, reckons 20–25, whereas Dan Rosen, Chairman of the Alliance of Angels in Seattle, goes for 12–30. Note that both have quite a range, so clearly nothing is absolute.

Yet another opinion puts the ideal portfolio size at a surprisingly precise 28, while Professor Richard Harrison of Edinburgh University claims that investing in 45 companies will give a good chance of a positive return. Then there are the statistics wizards who calculate that investing in 70 companies will give you a 90% chance of doubling your money (but it's still just a 'chance'), and having over 500 companies in your portfolio will make tripling your money 90% possible. I've even seen one claim that 90 investments will give a statistical chance of one with a 100x return – a unicorn exit. Buying a lottery ticket also has a statistical chance of a return but that statistical chance is remote, since the likelihood in the UK of winning the big prize is still around 14 million to 1.

Portfolio size is not just about statistics. The more companies you invest in, the less time you have to devote to each and the more time-consuming due diligence becomes. Somewhere, you'll have to find a happy medium where you're comfortable with the size of your portfolio and therefore the possible chances of success, and also with the amount of time you have available to put into those investments. Co-investing is crucial if you are to leverage and manage your investments efficiently, and we'll look at this in more detail later.

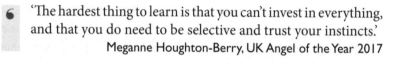

'The hardest thing to learn is that you can't invest in everything, and that you do need to be selective and trust your instincts.'
Meganne Houghton-Berry, UK Angel of the Year 2017

Following on

It is extremely rare for a business to reach profitability on the back of a single investment round. The only way this can happen is if customers provide the cash and very few new, scaling technology businesses can break even on sales in their first year or two. Indeed, very few businesses hit any of the targets in their business plan when they say they are going to, so they will need more money than originally anticipated. Founders are always optimistic and may plan for an exit in three to five years. This isn't nearly long enough. For most technology businesses, it takes 8–12 years before you see a return, although a really good business might see an exit in seven to ten years.

I should add that sometimes companies do exit before they reach profitability – either because they have great and defensible intellectual property (IP), such as the granted patents of a drug discovery company, or an 'acquihire' occurs. The latter is an acquisition that is made in order to hire the team and often involves some IP as well. This happens more often than you would imagine, and the exit value is generally £5–£15 million in the UK. If you have invested two or three times and the valuation on the ultimate round is now over the exit value, you will be losing money on some of your shares – probably a good result for the founders, who might make very low £ million, but not good for investors if they have invested at too high a valuation, which is one reason why invested investors are cautious about over-paying in any round.

> 'When you see a business plan, you need to see what the funding journey will look like. The plan will present Version 1 of the technology as the product, but we know Version 1 won't work, Version 2 probably won't work either, but Version 3 will, so the team has to look at that scenario.'
>
> Rajat Malhotra, 2013 UK Angel Investor of the Year and managing partner, Wren Capital

Since it takes a while to get to profitability and/or an exit, you should never invest all your capital in first rounds or you won't have any in reserve to follow on. You have to be prepared to stick with your investee company and follow your first investment with a second, and possibly third, round of a similar amount – or more, if you really believe in the progress.

If you and other investors don't follow on, there's a much greater chance that the company will fail because it runs out of money rather than because it isn't working out. If the company survives to exit, it may well have brought in additional investors along the way and you may find your shares have been diluted so much that your return drops to a minimal amount. You may also lose any say over the eventual outcome, as your vote will count for less (if anything) and other shareholders may vote for an exit that you think isn't right.

A 2014 report prepared by the British Business Bank for the Angel CoFund included a survey of investment rounds. While at least 80% of the companies included had four rounds, or fewer, there were some that went into double figures, including one that had 17 rounds of funding. Unfortunately, I don't know whether that was enough to reach an exit for that particular group of investors.

The message is, don't invest all your money at the start; always plan ahead for subsequent rounds.

> 'If I had been told at the beginning that I would have to put money into this company every year for six years, I would probably have said no. But look at it now – the team is fantastic and things are working well, so if I was asked to invest in it now, I'd say yes. So I was right – my six rounds were what the company needed to get to where it is today.'
>
> Simon Thorpe, invested investor

> Before you start working with your entrepreneurs, you have to find them. In the next chapter, we'll look at the best ways to meet founders, and other investors, and how to assess their ideas. I'll share my own investment criteria and how they help me to make the all-important decision of whether to invest or not. Am I in, or out?

INVESTED INVESTOR TAKEAWAY

- Being an invested investor is not easy and takes hard work.
- You have a lot to learn.
- Make sure you understand the risks associated with early stage investing.
- Build a portfolio.
- Keep money back for each of the companies in your portfolio so that you can follow on in later funding rounds.

AN INVESTOR'S STORY: 'GIVE IT TIME'

'This angel thing sounds interesting, I'll think I'll go and try it for a year. If it doesn't work out, I'll go back to being an accountant.'

It was 1 January 2000. Y2K had not destroyed all the computers in the world and Simon Blakey was sitting in a tiny office about to launch the next phase of his life as an invested investor.

'Right,' he thought to himself. 'I'm a business angel. Now what do I do?'

Today, the first piece of advice Simon would give any aspiring investor is to give it time. A year is barely long enough to have found, let alone made, the first deal, and exits typically come a decade or more later. But back in 2000, Simon didn't really know what he was letting himself in for.

Simon has a degree in biochemistry but having decided he didn't look good in a lab coat he trained as an accountant and had a successful career, first with Sainsbury's and later with Arthur Andersen, when he wanted to stretch himself beyond pure accountancy into consulting.

A spell as a property developer in London provided him with the resources to try angel investing and he decided to go into it full time, rather than as a weekend hobby. Eighteen years later, he has invested (alongside his brother Michael), in 28 companies, completed 69 funding rounds, and had eight profitable exits.

Simon is happy to admit that he relied heavily on the experience of other people in the early days, and that's typical of most invested investors. He started by talking to as many people as he could to try and work out what angel investing was all about.

When Simon started his investment journey, the dotcom boom was reaching its peak and all the money was rushing into anything with '.com' in its name. But Simon felt the business model for dotcom companies was weak and saw money rushing in to fund ideas with very little commercial substance. He made the key decision to invest in unfashionable businesses with 'unfashionable', i.e. low, valuations.

A wise decision, as it turned out. Angel investing is as prone to the latest trends as anything else in life, and there have been plenty of 'next big things' since the dotcom bubble burst. Social networks were all the rage a few years ago but then they were superseded by apps, which then lost out when marketplaces became the next buzzword. And now everyone wants the next Initial Coin Offering (ICO), machine learning (although they always call it 'AI' to make it sound sexier) or blockchain story.

In 2001, just after the sales of 3G licences in the UK, telecommunications companies went out of fashion, and Simon found his first unfashionable investment – a telco company. Against the norm, it proved to be one of his shortest investment journeys, exiting a mere 18 months later. Now he understands how unusual that is – and two of his more recent successful exits have been 13 and 17 years in the making (but worth the wait, with both returning many multiples after a single initial investment).

For Simon, the underlying business model is far more important than the latest investing craze. What is the problem the product is solving, and will people pay for it? If there's a viable route to monetisation, then it's a deal worth looking at. And once the deal is done, he is very involved with the company as it grows, either as a Board member or Board observer, and always as a willing and sympathetic ear.

And what if he hadn't had any early exits to whet his appetite? Perhaps he would have given up and never reached the stage where he can advise any new investors to 'give it time'.

CHAPTER 3

Funder meets founder

So you still want to be an angel investor, even though you know it won't be easy and you could well lose your money. You're pretty sure there are some founders out there who need funding. But where are you going to find them? And how are you going to pick the right ones to invest in? I believe both sides, investors and entrepreneurs, share equal responsibilities when it comes to initiating and developing a productive relationship.

Making contact

As with any relationship, there are plenty of ways for you to meet entrepreneurs. The world of angel investing and entrepreneurship is well served by the equivalents of internet dating, speed dating and networking opportunities. Introductions can be made through angel groups and by attending events. Later, you may find you also get involved in mentoring and accelerator programmes.

First, always remember that you want to meet people from all parts of the start-up ecosystem – not only other angels, but also entrepreneurs, founders, advisors and others involved in helping businesses get started and grow. The same goes if you're an entrepreneur reading this book to find out how angels tick – it's a community and you need to know everyone involved.

> Beware chemistry. I have an investor friend who says, 'If it's love at first sight, walk away'. Ideas and people can be very attractive but you mustn't let your heart rule your head when making investment decisions.

The best way to meet a founder is through an introduction from another, trusted investor, someone whose judgement you respect and who understands your reasons for getting into angel investing. It's the equivalent of an endorsement, and is self-policing. Angels you know and respect would not introduce you to someone who wasn't worth getting to know, otherwise you might not do the same for them in the future.

An ideal start would be to find a local angel who guides and sponsors you through the process but who is also part of a group, so you can learn from the experiences of everyone in the group. There's strength in numbers, so joining a group gives you some reassurance that you're not stepping into the unknown.

Saying 'Look for a local angel' is all very well, but if you're a brand new investor with no portfolio as yet, you probably don't know any other angels, so how do you start?

Investor groups are a good place to find out what's going on in your area and, as always, the internet is a good place to start looking for them. I'm on the Board of the UK Business Angels Association, UKBAA, and members include syndicates and angel networks as well as individuals. There are numerous UKBAA events during the year, including regional and sector-specific events – such as the Investment Catalyst event, where the UKBAA teams up with the Royal Society of Chemistry to showcase start-ups innovating in chemical science.

I recommend finding your local angel investing network, if there is one, or a regional group if there isn't anything closer to hand. That way, you can start slowly, learn the ropes and meet fellow investors in your area and your sector. There are over 100 angel groups in the UK. You can find a good number on the latest list on the UKBAA website and also learn where the different groups are active. Do find out as much as you can about the group and its methods before plunging in, as they are often slightly different and you will probably have a preference for the type of people you want to invest with and the type of companies you want to invest in.

If you're based outside the UK, the European Business Angel Network, EBAN (of which I am president) might be the place to start. EBAN members represent over 60 countries and territories, extending beyond Europe to the US, New Zealand, Brazil and elsewhere. The US also has its own business angel ecosystem and, again, a quick search will no doubt reveal groups local to where you are.

It's not just angel groups that can help you get to know the landscape. The British Business Bank runs roadshows for funders and businesses looking to start up or scale up, and there are plenty of other sources of information and events.

But don't forget – you are never forced to invest. Don't automatically leap to put your money into the first company your new associates suggest; take the time to make up your own mind about whether it's a good fit for you, something we'll look at more closely in the next chapter.

Events are another good way to meet people and start building your contacts. There are numerous networking and funding organisations helping to promote young and growing companies around the UK, and I'm willing to bet that there's probably an event where funders and entrepreneurs could meet just about every night somewhere in the country. Watch out for 'pitchfests', though. An event that consists of a series of pitches to an audience of, say, 200 people doesn't really work because there are too many people for any meaningful interactions. You can't get close to someone and get a real sense of who they are if they're up on a stage and you're sitting back in the stalls. That said, you may find something that is interesting enough that you want to arrange a follow-up meeting, so keep an open mind.

Events will always have a networking element but don't expect that to be the answer. You'll meet plenty of entrepreneurs – they'll practically queue up to talk to you given half a chance – but it's hard for them to deliver a worthwhile pitch when approaching you over drinks. Yes, every entrepreneur is told to have their elevator pitch ready for that accidental meeting with a famous investor in a lift, but in a crowded room with a lot of noise and perhaps a group of people standing around wanting to talk to you, all they can hope for is that they give enough useful information to make you want to continue the conversation. The situation is hardly conducive to concentration, let alone sensible analysis of what is being described, so they'll have to have something special to say if you're not going to dump their business card in the bin on the way out.

One of my earliest investments began very inauspiciously. I was mentoring start-ups on an accelerator programme and went along to an informal pitching event. One of the entrepreneurs had an interesting career behind him already and had been wondering whether to follow his father into law. But now he had learned how to program and was full of enthusiasm for his new venture. In fact, he was so full of enthusiasm that his mouth was way ahead of his brain, rattling out ideas and plans almost incoherently.

'There's no way I could ever invest in this guy', I thought. 'He's completely unbackable. How could he explain things to his tech team, let alone a customer?'

Luckily, that very enthusiastic entrepreneur listened to advice – from me and others – and got his thoughts and messages under control. To the extent that my opinion of him switched completely. In fact, his transformation was so successful that I became the lead investor for the first round of funding for his company seven years ago and remain on the Board today.

Be prepared to deal with the cold call

Another way to find potential investees is to have them find you but this can be inefficient, and you need to know more about what you're doing before you put yourself out there for strangers to find.

I rarely follow up and invest in someone who contacts me out of the blue. I have a website, as do some other angels, and I realise that by having a website and announcing what I do to the world, I lay myself open to contacts from strangers. Not surprisingly, I get emails and LinkedIn contacts from people I've never met. But being approached 'cold' like that is more likely to turn me off than pique my interest. And it's not hard to meet me in person, as I go to perhaps 100 events every year.

I also have a very specific set of investment criteria listed on my website, which we'll get to shortly as they form the backbone of my decision-making. I have developed these criteria over years of investing and if an entrepreneur gets in touch with me without having bothered to read them, or even when they have read them and know they don't meet the criteria, it's pretty easy to say, 'no'.

In fact, it's always easier to say 'no' than 'yes', because 'yes' means more work, so an entrepreneur would have to offer something pretty special to get past 'no'. But always be polite and helpful when saying 'no' – you never know where that entrepreneur might turn up again, and as I mentioned earlier, someone I originally thought was unbackable is turning out to be a star.

As an invested investor, you are always aware of whether or not an entrepreneur who approaches you has done their homework. Have they looked at your investment criteria, if these are in the public domain? Or have they found out about you in other ways, for instance via LinkedIn or an article that you were quoted in, to make sure that you're the right person to approach? Have they observed your social media activity and chosen the most appropriate channel to contact you? If the entrepreneur can't assess and qualify potential investors, they may not be much better at qualifying potential customers, a point worth thinking about.

Many investors have a list of entrepreneurs and other angels that they have learned to steer clear of, and you want to avoid joining that list at all costs.

> There was one time I gave a polite refusal and pointed out that the emailer should have checked his plan against my investment criteria before sending, as his company clearly wasn't what I was looking for. He had the cheek (although I admired his hustling) to email back and say he was just trying to get a reaction out of me! If he gets in touch again, I'll probably take a look at his business plan.

ENTREPRENEUR TAKEAWAY

Do your homework on potential investors and try and research and meet them in person first if you can. They'll appreciate your efforts and be more willing to listen to what you have to say.

Developing your investment criteria

You will need to develop a set of investment criteria to help you decide when to invest. These will cover a multitude of factors, from the skills and experience of the founding team to the type of product and the sector they are planning to operate in. The business model and management will also be important, as will any elements particular to your areas of expertise. I specialise in the technology sector and so my investment criteria are geared towards the particular challenges that I know tech start-ups have to address.

My investment criteria guide my thinking from first impressions through to actually making an investment, and also provide the basis for my due diligence. They provide me with a number of points where I will say 'no' if things aren't right. Don't forget, these are *my* criteria, developed over years of experience as an entrepreneur and invested investor. You must develop your own rules for investing and decide how important the different factors are to you.

My criteria for investing in technology start-ups

The team
- High growth ambitions
- Outstanding team of at least two people
- UK legal structure
- Founders based in the UK
- Deep trust and respect for the investor director (whether they are yet to be chosen or already in post)
- Understanding of the ratio between customer lifetime value (CLV) and cost of customer acquisition (CCA)

The product
- Evidence of a large market
- Defensibility
- In technology (my sector)
- B2B or (rarely) B2B2C
- Deep product technology

The finances
- Early stage income
- Pre-money valuation up to a maximum of £2 million
- Plan for a minimum 10x valuation increase over 4–10 years
- No platforms that charge fees
- Syndicated
- Very few non-disclosure agreements (NDAs)

I'm going to talk you through my investment criteria so you can understand better why I apply them. This will help you to think about what factors might be important to you and how to start developing them into a set of rules to help guide your own investments.

My investment criteria – the team

You've probably heard the old adage about it being better to back a brilliant team with a mediocre idea than a mediocre team with a brilliant idea, and all my experience points to that adage being true. Angels invest in people. My first interest when looking at a business idea is to check the team behind it.

There are some key factors that I think are essential in any successful team, and I've turned down many business plans in minutes – all it took was a quick glance at the team and I knew they weren't for me. I've had business plans that didn't even mention the team, let alone cite any relevant business credentials and experience. Those plans went straight in the bin. If the team isn't worth mentioning, it's definitely not worth investing in.

High growth ambitions Otherwise why bother? But it's not a given – not every team of entrepreneurs thinks beyond making a comfortable profit and working sensible hours, often termed a lifestyle business. There are investors who are quite happy to fund such businesses and enjoy an income from the dividends they produce, but that's not the type of investment I want to make. I want to know if the founders have the drive to create something bigger, even if that means risking the business itself. No guts, no glory. If the founders don't have high growth ambitions, they may well not be able to deliver the return I need for taking the risk of backing them. So I want to know if they have a plan of how to get to market, what their target date is for profitability, and how they will spend my money to reach their ambitious goals.

An outstanding team of two or three people Sole founders find it difficult to get investment from business angels and might be better off going down the crowdfunding route, or the three Fs. Two is good for me, so is three, but four is too many.

❝   Why four founders is too many – for me
I don't like to invest where there are four or more co-founders for several reasons. First, they'll need a bigger pie. If we're talking about founding a business that will eventually yield life-changing sums of money for the founders (which is the typical expectation), the exit valuation will have to be high enough to provide that amount for four people rather than two or three. With dilutions along the way, that puts pressure on getting a high valuation at exit and often corresponds to higher valuations on the first round.

With four founders, skill sets will overlap, so essentially one (or more) of them may be 'redundant' because their skills are duplicated in the other members of the team. In addition, there's a higher chance of one of the founders changing their mind and wanting out, and that causes pain and all sorts of issues around unwinding the shares and restructuring to get the company moving forward again.

When I look at a pitch deck, I expect the team to be on the second slide, and my first question is, 'Are these people going to be backable?' I'll look at a number of factors related to the team but in particular their experience, their qualifications, whether they've worked together before and, if not, how they know each other now.

I want to know if they bring big corporate or an entrepreneurial background to the team. Although useful, I'm not so fussed about MBAs, but I do want to make sure that the chief technology officer (CTO) has the right technical expertise. If they've worked together before, the fact that they're willing to do it again is a good sign. If they haven't worked together before, I like to understand if they've joined together based on a shared vision, or they've been put together by one of the founders and may take time to develop a unity of vision and a strong working relationship.

I have to confess that I also look at their ages. I know people in their seventies who are still starting companies – and here am I, in my early sixties, launching what often feels like a risky start-up with the Invested Investor project. If they've been doing it all their lives, older entrepreneurs know the ins and outs of growing a business and the amount of work they're letting themselves in for. Younger entrepreneurs may be lacking in experience but they should be willing to learn.

I'd be less keen to back someone who suddenly decides to try being an entrepreneur for the first time in their fifties or sixties. It's not ageism; it's a question of whether they meet my criteria for investment. Sad to say, they may well be going down the start-up route because they've been made redundant and can't find another job. It's unlikely that they'll have the right experience, and I know how hard it is to start a business even when you do have experience.

I prefer it when the grey hair is on the heads of the investors and the advisors, not the entrepreneurs and founders.

UK legal structure I understand and am bound by the UK legal structure, so it makes sense to stick with what I know. Under UK law and HMRC rules, there are various tax efficiencies for investors. These currently fall into four categories: the Enterprise Investment Scheme (EIS), Seed Enterprise Investment Scheme (SEIS), Social Investment Tax Relief (SITR) and Venture Capital Trust (VCT), and entrepreneurs need to understand these just as much as investors.

However, investors must not expect to get tax relief on exit; in fact, you may end up repaying tax refunds if the exit is too early or does not qualify. I have invested several times where tax reliefs were not available and have had, and expect more, exits where at least some of my investment does not fit in with EIS rules. The most common reason investments are disqualified from tax relief is because the exit occurs less than three years after the most recent round. I know one investor who had to pay millions in tax because the exit came just a few weeks too soon.

> ❛ Don't invest for tax reasons – don't let the tax tail wag the dog. But do maximise any tax benefits available, as they can make a significant difference to portfolio outcomes over time.

Founders based in the UK Having founders based in the UK is important because otherwise it's much harder for me to be an invested investor.

I feel it's very important to meet the founders face-to-face from the early stages, not least if I'm going to make a sensible decision about whether I want to go on this very risky journey with them. I'll meet them before I even decide to start on that journey, and then again during due diligence, and probably once or twice a year after that if I'm not on the Board, so they mustn't be too far away.

It's simple maths. If you are going to take an active role in some of your portfolio companies, even if you don't attend Board meetings, you don't want to spend half your time on the road. If you live in Edinburgh and invest in a company in Exeter, keeping your part of the investment bargain will involve a seven-hours-plus train journey each way, and may cost several hundred pounds. Multiply that by a minimum of two or three meetings per year, and you can see that it doesn't make a lot of sense.

I strongly prefer my investments to be within a 90-minute rail journey from where I live near Cambridge. Anything further than that and I end up spending too much time travelling to and from the company and not enough time adding value. Although I enjoy driving, I can't justify long-distance taxi rides and we all know the dangers of not concentrating on the road.

Having said that, yes, I do have investments in companies based in York, Bulgaria and California, none of which is 90 minutes away from my house by train, helicopter or any other means of transport. But the company in York is a legacy from my early life, and the companies in Bulgaria and California were nearby originally; they simply moved to a better location for the business. I keep in touch with them but face-to-face meetings are very rare.

Deep trust and respect for the investor director It's impossible to be actively involved in all the companies in your portfolio all the time. If I'm not leading the investment or on the Board, I want to know that my representative from the investor group, the investor director, has my interests in mind, and everyone else's, and represents us in the way we would ourselves. We'll look at the importance of communication later in this book, but this is one of the starting points for building trust and transparency into the process.

Understanding CLV:CCA This is the ratio between customer lifetime value (CLV) and cost of customer acquisition (CCA), and is important in the tech sector (but not so for biotech start-ups). If the founders don't understand this fundamental concept, they may not have a head for business between them.

CLV is defined as the entire predicted gross profit over the life-time of a relationship with a customer – capture a customer and keep them for a long time, and the profits will add up. CCA, as its name suggests, is how much it costs you to capture that customer in the first place. It is the sum of all sales and marketing expenses divided by the number of new customers added. On the surface, it seems fairly straightforward – if the company spends a total of £X on sales and marketing, which includes not only obvious costs like copywriting, printing, website design and videos, but also sales and marketing salaries, travel, administration and a host of other things, and ends up with Y new customers as a result, then the cost per customer is X/Y. At this point, the entrepreneur might think they can decide whether the sales and marketing budget was worth it based on that answer. But with many products, the sale is only the beginning, and there may be ongoing contracts for servicing, maintenance, updates and consultancy to factor into the calculations. Understanding this, and the metrics to evaluate it, is crucial.

Personally I like to see a CLV of at least 8–10 times the CCA. And do remember if you have a platform or market place, both sides have a CLV and CCA. Facebook or Twitter do not charge us as users but they still have to source and support us.

Some entrepreneurs misunderstand gross margin/contribution and revenue when calculating CLV. Revenue is of no interest to me. 'Revenue is vanity, profit is sanity – cash is reality', as they say. Revenues can be high but margins small, and profitability therefore low, if the cost of each sale is high, and that's particularly the case with a single sale to one customer.

Buyers who only buy once are expensive. Imagine you're selling a puppy. You have to invest in advertisements, evidence of pedigree and vets' fees to get the puppy vaccinated and chipped so it can leave home. Your customer buys one puppy from you and never comes back. That's an expensive sale because you've spent all that money to sell one puppy, and you can only sell it once. If you have a litter of, say, five puppies, the cost per sale doesn't come down much because the only cost that can be shared across all five puppies is the advertising; the other costs are the same for each puppy.

Now if the people who bought those puppies from you liked them so much they come back again a few years later when you have another litter for sale, the cost of customer acquisition has gone down, as you haven't had to advertise for them, but the other selling costs remain. In the meantime, you've kept the puppies' mother housed and fed, paid her vet bills and possibly a stud fee. You're beginning to wonder why you went into the puppy business.

Unlike puppies and other one-off sales, your founders may be selling a product or service that has not only ongoing costs but also ongoing revenues, such as a subscription, upgrades or client fees. Indeed, our puppy breeder could have a more stable business if they also started selling dog food, and offered grooming and walking services. Now the length of time a customer stays becomes much more important to overall profitability.

Calculating the lifetime value of a customer is useful because it helps to predict the total gross profit over the entire lifetime of the relationship with a particular customer – and hence helps the entrepreneur to decide whether spending all that money on marketing to attract new customers was worth it. Will they bring in more gross profit over time than it costs to acquire them? Churn rate (how quickly customers are lost) and average revenue per customer come into the equation. Should they spend more on customer retention? And remember, the early adopter customers will be easier (and hence cheaper) to find and be more flexible with product issues. Don't let this mislead you.

Having such forward-looking metrics is important not only for short-term budgeting, but also when seeking additional funding for growth. It also helps entrepreneurs to segment their customers, so they put more effort – and investment – into those who will bring most benefit to the business over the long term. As an investor, you want to be confident that the entrepreneurs you are backing understand this all-important concept.

My investment criteria – the product

You'll see that these are geared very much towards the tech sector and some may not be applicable to you, but most will indicate areas of general interest if not specific concern.

Evidence of a large market I'd classify a large market as worth globally at least 100 million pounds, dollars or euros, although not all businesses need to have global ambitions. Note that I don't need to see a billion-plus market – angels can get an excellent return even if the investee company's revenues are less than £5 million on exit. By evidence, I mean recent data from respected sources, not a media headline announcing the next big thing.

Defensibility The sector you invest in will determine how important defensibility and patents are to your investment decisions. In some sectors, such as life sciences, patents are essential. For most technology start-ups, patent applications are good, patents filed and granted much better. However, the patents might not be that valuable – there are ways other companies can get round patents, and they can be costly to defend, not only in cash but also in the amount of time taken up. The key question comes down to freedom to operate – are there other companies with patents in the same space that could challenge the core technology of the business? We'll come back to patents later, but it's worth pointing out that defensibility could also be about speed to market or sector know-how. If there is nothing about any of these in the business plan, I'm unlikely to follow up.

My sector   It makes a huge amount of sense to invest in things that you understand. I have strong experience in software, electronics, RF communications, sensing and related areas. I have limited knowledge of life science technology, although medical technology is usually ok – and you'll see that it's sometimes possible to invest outside your core sector if you have fellow investors with the right knowledge, so this isn't a totally exclusive rule. For instance, I have invested in a therapeutics company, Exonate, which intends to help sufferers of wet macular degeneration. The normal treatment is an injection in the eye every few weeks, but Exonate is working on a new therapy that can be administered as eye drops. I have no clue how the molecules will get through the eyeball nor how they will work when they reach the retina, but I have huge faith in the team and the board. I recommend potential investees look at my portfolio to get an idea of whether their start-up is a good fit for me.

B2B or (rarely) B2B2C   Again, this is a question of investing in what you know. I've spent most of my life in B2B and that is where I'm comfortable and have useful contacts for my investees. I have founded two B2C start-ups (one in tech and the other speculatively building houses) and did not enjoy communicating with consumers, who seem to confuse price (what I wanted to charge) with value (what the product was worth to them). And I know I am also a consumer!

I say 'never' to B2C because my experience of B2C is extremely limited, and the customer acquisition cost of a consumer seems to me to be a black art. So I won't necessarily be able to add much value to a B2C proposition, although it's just possible I might be tempted into B2C if I know the team personally and believe in them. The astute among you will note that writing and selling this book is a B2C venture – but I'm aiming for this project to simply break even, not generate J K Rowling levels of sales.

Deep product technology I'm clear about what I don't invest in. I don't invest in web or mobile apps, or service businesses. I will invest in a platform, provided there is a clear understanding of the costs of sourcing/supporting and monetisation of both sides of the platform – the CLV:CAC described above.

My investment criteria – the finances

Investors want to be reassured that their money is going to be used wisely and directed towards providing something that customers will pay for. I look for a solid grasp of the important basics and an understanding of my needs as an investor. A great vision under-pinned by financial realism tells me that even if the team has its head in the clouds, it also has its feet on the ground.

Early stage income Ideally I'd like to see the company pre-revenue, although evidence of valid customer sales traction, even if it's a one-off trial, could help.

There are various ways founders might claim income but some-times deeper scrutiny reveals a few cracks. An order from a big company does not validate the product – it's always possible to find someone who is permitted to sign off a small order, say for £5–10k; it could even be someone the founder used to work with doing them a favour. It is much harder to make the connection and close a bigger sale with someone higher up. And small orders are often not 'real' sales, just a way for the purchaser to get a look at the technology and try it out. There is no guarantee that they'll come back for more.

Trials are also often given as evidence for future income. But a free trial is absolutely not the same as a paying customer and the former will not necessarily lead to the latter. A paid trial is better – the company has now become a supplier to the customer. This is more of a commitment and may well have taken months to achieve. However, even a paid trial can be misleading, as some industries tend to back multiple trials before selecting a winner, and so it is no guarantee of future income.

Pre-money valuation This is the valuation of the company before an investment or funding round, and my target range is from less than £1 million, with an upper limit of £2 million, unless the company is exceptional. Valuations have been moving upwards due to what I see as the over-supply of early stage money, particularly in London, and not (yet?) because exits are at a larger multiple or more frequent. We'll look at valuations more closely in Chapter 5.

Minimum 10x valuation increase over 4–10 years This is what most angels would hope for. Say a company's ownership is 750 shares and the founders issue 250 shares, at £1,000 per share, in a funding round. They have gained a total investment in the company of £250,000 and valued the company at £1 million because the other 750 shares are now, theoretically, also worth £1,000 each. If there are no follow-on rounds, and so no dilution, and the company is sold for £10 million, then 25% of the company is now worth £2.5 million, that is, 10 times the initial investment. If you are asking for a £1 million post-investment valuation, what does your company look like? And who will buy it for £10+ million in a few years' time?

No platforms that charge fees I want direct contact with the founders. Although I understand that everyone has to live, I am not keen on co-investing with early stage syndicates or funds that take a fee. Fees might be charged for pitching, raising the target amount successfully or monitoring the board, or even all three, but I prefer to be involved in all of those activities directly rather than pay for them to be provided through a third party.

Syndicated I never invest alone. If I like a proposition, I may build a syndicate from scratch if necessary (this is deal leading, which we'll look at in Chapter 5). Invested investors want and expect to add value with connections, advice, governance and future funding, and syndicates mean that there is more of that added value available to help the company. Syndication to me is not the same as crowdfunding because it involves a much smaller and much more connected group. I don't invest in any deals that have been, or are, on any equity crowdfunding site except some via Syndicate Room, which has a different model from other platforms (and in which I am an investor).

Very few non-disclosure agreements The only time I will sign a non-disclosure agreement (NDA) is if an entrepreneur wants to show me an un-filed patent during due diligence. This is my answer to a problem I have come up against in the past but it might not be so crucial for you as a new investor developing your own investment criteria.

Non-disclosure agreements are not always applicable but they can be particularly important for me when investing in the technology sector. Nonetheless, they are often difficult, as it can be hard to strike a balance between what I as an investor need to know and what an entrepreneur feels they need to protect.

I have seen over 8,000 business plans in the last decade, some of which, not surprisingly, are very similar. If I had signed NDAs for even a few of them, I might not have been permitted to look at some of the others. A lack of NDAs shouldn't bring the budding relationship to a grinding halt. If the lack of an NDA seems to be a deal-breaker, the entrepreneur might want to seek outside advice on what they can safely disclose.

> **ENTREPRENEUR TAKEAWAY**
>
> If you're an entrepreneur reading this and think I sound a bit harsh, please don't be discouraged. We are all, investors and entrepreneurs alike, working towards the same goals. We are all extremely passionate about what we do. Seeking to understand each others' motives and reasons for the decisions we make is one way to promote greater transparency – and reach better deals based on better information.

The pitch deck

Your ideal pitch deck should reflect your own investment criteria. Assuming the entrepreneurs have access to your criteria, they ought to put together a pitch deck that answers your requirements and makes it easier for you to decide whether to get further involved. Given that my investment criteria are clearly stated on my website, you'd think that the people who contact me out of the blue would have an easy time putting together a pitch deck that hits all the right notes, but that isn't always the case.

> I've just received a 57-page pitch deck (which is 40+ pages too long for first contact) and the team is not mentioned until slide 40. Email deleted.

A good pitch deck hits all the key points that will make me want to find out more. Just like the classic elevator pitch, if it doesn't grab me in a few slides, I'm not going to waste my time on it. I can dismiss a business plan in minutes, and frequently do. This may sound arrogant but an invested investor will see hundreds of deal opportunities every year and typically invest in fewer than ten, so they need a filter process. The next stage takes time and energy, so I have to have a strong feeling that it'll be worth the work.

If I'm listening to a pitch, I'd expect to see 10–15 slides, plus a few ancillary slides for questions. If it is being emailed to me in the first instance, along with the 10–15 slides I'd expect a few appendix slides (if needed) to expand on data such as market size or cost of customer acquisition.

The same pitch deck won't work on stage and via email. A common problem with pitch decks is their suitability for the medium of delivery. That's a posh way of saying that pitch decks delivered on stage to an audience should be mostly images, charts and graphs, whereas a deck emailed to a potential investor should be mostly words – that is, the bullet-point narrative that would be delivered on stage. You can't make a decision to explore a company more deeply based on a bunch of pretty pictures with no one there to explain what they mean.

Pitches are also living documents, so they should be dated and have a version number – again, as an invested investor you're looking for founders who understand what you need and are organised and efficient enough to deliver it in the appropriate format.

What I like to see in a pitch deck

Slide 1   Images of market and/or product and/or team, with company name/logo, mission, vision

Slide 2   Team – photos, education, background; any non-executive directors or advisors who have already been appointed or are guaranteed to be appointed after the round closes

Slide 3   The unmet need. Could be an illustration of business/consumer journey containing problem that needs solving

Slide 4   Your solution

5–10 ancillary slides covering:
- Market size – bottom up, rather than top down (selling to 0.1% of all mobile phone users is a big number, but not credible)
- Route to market
- Competition
- Pricing
- Cost of customer acquisition and customer lifetime value
- Finances 1: use of investment capital over the 12–18 months to the next round
- Finances 2: three- or five-year plan with sales, gross margin, overheads and losses/profits (Investors rarely believe this, and it will be wrong anyway, but it shows you have thought through the longer term. A simple graph will suffice)
- Defensibility
- Product (not service, although some products may have an element of service income, for instance customisation and/or maintenance)
- Progress to date if you are already trading
- Exit planning (again, rarely correct, but shows you intend to exit)

Final slide   Overview of team, market, tech and financial (or other) 'ask'

The exceptions to the rule

As you'll have noticed, I have investment criteria but they're not necessarily hard and fast rules. There are always exceptions, and if I followed my criteria too slavishly, I might miss out on a great opportunity. You have to learn to allow for a certain level of imperfection, and over time you'll get a sense of where you can be more relaxed and where you really have to stick to the criteria you've established.

One exception was a young Portuguese man who joined the Ignite programme at Cambridge Judge Business School after completing his MBA. Gonçalo de Vasconcelos wanted to build a platform for angel investors and approached me as part of his research. I wasn't interested in investing at the beginning, because what he was suggesting was well outside my investment criteria. But after long discussions, where he proved he was a good listener, I put a small amount into his 'family and friends' round. It didn't take much longer for Gonçalo to convince me that what he was doing would work with Syndicate Room.

The angels I co-invest and work with all have their own sets of criteria around essentially the same topics, but they may be more or less stringent about them, for instance, how far they might stray from familiar sectors, and how much reliance they might put on market size. They may also be more relaxed about the locations of their investee companies – if they already have investments in another part of the country or overseas, they may be comfortable with the amount of travel involved because they can cover several companies in one visit – or they may have confidence in the investor directors involved in these companies on their behalf.

What's most important about the angels I co-invest with is that I know and trust them – so sometimes, I might relax my own requirements because I know what their criteria are and know that they are being guided appropriately. The level of trust means that I know it's ok to follow them when I think their investment criteria are more valid than mine.

> You've met some founders, you've applied a few checks and balances based on advice from fellow angels and your own investment criteria (which are probably still under development), and you're keen to get on and hand over the money (the money that you can afford to lose, remember). But if you're going to be an invested investor, you're still a long way from signing on the dotted line. Next up, due diligence.

INVESTED INVESTOR TAKEAWAY

- Build a broad and deep network of contacts from all parts of the ecosystem.
- Develop a set of investment criteria that work for you.
- Create your own ideal pitch deck template to help assess those sent to you.
- Don't be too inflexible and miss an opportunity because it isn't a perfect fit.

AN ENTREPRENEUR'S STORY:
The dinner party conversation and the £2.3 billion company

Jonathan Milner and his girlfriend, Rosy, moved to Cambridge when her dream job came up. Having taken his first degree, in applied biology, at Bath University, Milner had completed a PhD at Leicester, where he met Rosy, and the two of them had gone to Bath for his post-doc. Now she had been offered a job with a Cambridge art gallery, and Jonathan was hoping to get his own dream job with Cambridge Antibody Technology, better known as CAT. Unfortunately, the interview was a disaster and his dream was dashed.

Time for plan B, and Jonathan spotted an opportunity in the lab run by cancer specialist Professor Tony Kouzarides. He felt underqualified, but applied anyway. He and Kouzarides hit it off so well he was offered the job, despite Kouzarides later admitting that he hadn't looked at Jonathan's CV.

After three years working with Kouzarides on breast cancer research, Milner was starting to think about his next step. His father had been an entrepreneur and he was thinking of going down the entrepreneurial route himself, but had yet to come up with a business idea.

It was a chat in the pub that sowed the first seeds for Abcam. Luke Hughes-Davis, a medical researcher, remarked how he 'couldn't stand' the antibodies he was having to use for his research. Jonathan had what he describes as an 'entrepreneurial seizure', and the two of them started to think how they could set up a company making antibodies. They had some rather far-fetched ideas to begin with, but these didn't get them any closer to a proper business plan.

Then serendipity stepped in. Ros Cleevely, who owned the art gallery where Rosy worked, decided to have a Christmas dinner for the staff and their partners. Jonathan sat opposite Ros' husband, David, and began a conversation that would change his life. To David's question as to his career plans, Jonathan replied that he was thinking of setting up a business. Unknown to him, David was an entrepreneur himself and an active participant in Cambridge's entrepreneurial tech community.

David asked Jonathan how much it cost to make one unit of antibody but he couldn't answer so they went through it from first principles. At £1,500 per animal and up to 500 units, £3 was the answer. On hearing each unit sold for £150 to £200, David thought there was something wrong; maybe there was a problem with shipping? But Jonathan explained the antibodies could survive two to three days in the post, and David got interested – that meant you could sell via a website and deliver to anywhere. Jonathan later admitted he had yet to point out the risk: predicting which antibodies would be popular was extremely difficult, so many different types had to be manufactured even though they might not lead to sales. He didn't know that David had already discounted that and was still impressed with the potential margin.

The upshot was that David invited Jonathan to come and have a more detailed chat about his business ideas the following Saturday, starting a pattern that was to prove the foundation for Jonathan's transition from academic to entrepreneur.

But that first session almost led nowhere. Jonathan could see that his rather more out-there ideas, involving Luke's uncle's sheep farm in

Wales, were not getting a positive response as David felt the risk of a high fixed-cost base was too great.

Nevertheless, the two continued to meet on Saturday mornings. Now it got down to whether Jonathan had any money to put into his putative company. 'No', was the obvious answer – he was a lowly paid researcher and he and Rosy had just taken out a mortgage to buy their first house, so there was no cash to spare.

Invested investors often say that gut instinct tells them a lot about entrepreneurs, but that sometimes you have to test that instinct before you invest. David decided it was time to test Jonathan. He explained that he was willing to invest, but that Jonathan had to raise some cash himself. If he couldn't do that, David would back off.

One week later, Jonathan turned up with a cheque for £11,000, having remortgaged his new house. David knew this was nowhere near enough, but the effort demonstrated Jonathan's commitment, and his first investment of £40,000 in Abcam was secured. David's company, Analysys, provided the web development.

The fledgling company had a few scares along the way, including the time when, two weeks away from running out of cash, Jonathan famously resorted to visiting all the labs he knew in Cambridge with an ice bucket full of antibodies, hoping to make some sales. Although nobody was willing to buy, they did tell him which antibodies they needed and asked if he could supply them. Naturally he said yes, and the result was the start of a contract antibody business, which generated the cash the company needed to find its feet.

The next squeaky moment was the night before their website was due to go live, when the site was still only plans and ideas on paper. An all-nighter with the web developer got them over that hurdle, and soon, with the help of Muscat, a search engine provided by David's contact John Snyder, incorporated into the website, they were gathering valuable information about which antibodies were searched for most often and who wanted them.

This information, coupled with the introduction of product reviews, would prove pivotal in the company's success. Initially, the website linked out to other providers of antibodies when Abcam could not supply what was wanted; but knowing their customers as well as they did, they soon created their own catalogue of the most desirable antibodies.

Allowing product reviews on the site was an innovation that added another dimension. We're used to online reviews of just about anything we purchase today, but back in the 1990s and early 2000s, this was novel, and indeed frowned on in the scientific community. But detailed information about the temperature, pH and other conditions under which the antibodies had been used was critical for other researchers working with the same antibodies, and added value to Abcam's offering.

Abcam had taken only around £450,000 in funding to start the business and launch the website but in 2001, it ran out of money and the VCs refused to invest. David raided his pension fund and bailed out the company with a further £420,000. From then on, Abcam continued to grow successfully on customer money until the company was floated on AIM in October 2005, with a market capitalisation of around £50 million. Today, the company has a market capitalisation of around £2.3 billion.

CHAPTER 4

Due diligence

Finding a team with a business plan that shows some promise is just the first step on a long road. It may be 8–10 years before you find out whether or not you're going to get a good return on your investment, so you'd better start out as you mean to go on – and that takes a lot of hard work at the beginning. If you and your entrepreneurs are going to last the distance, you have to be sure about them and they have to be sure about you. Let's talk about due diligence.

The transparency issue

I can't stress this enough – everyone involved in setting up and funding a new company must be open and transparent from the start, otherwise things are almost certain to go wrong down the line, and the fallout could have severe repercussions, especially where large sums of money are involved.

❝ 'We didn't think you needed to know about that,' is the wrong thing to say.

Entrepreneurs are naturally wary when selling a share in their company to a relative stranger. They're frightened of losing control of their business, and suspect that all investors are nasty people who will rule the board and only have their own interests in mind. I've heard it said that entrepreneurs who have been running a profitable company for many years would rather sell their grandmother than sell shares to an investor and have them on their board. *Dragons' Den* has done nothing to help the situation – even though entrepreneurs going on the programme know that they are there to sell some of their business. It's designed as entertainment, so the programmes are edited to make the process seem highly confrontational and antagonistic. The so-called dragons are often shown humiliating the entrepreneurs until they crack under the pressure and sell far more of their business than they intended to. This is not, or should not be, what happens in the real world.

Invested investors are also wary because they're about to give a group of founders a large amount of money, so they want to be as sure as is humanly possible that they are making the right decision. They will have to ask questions about all aspects of the company and the team, but the point is to build a working relationship, not to score points.

Entrepreneurs, especially those starting a business for the first time, need reassurance that, as an invested investor, you will be friendly, supportive and add value to the business. Being open and transparent is the first step to achieving this. Naturally, you will expect the entrepreneurs to be open and transparent with you, as well – and if they're not, they're giving you an easy way to say 'no' before you've gone very far with them, and possibly damaging their chances of finding investment elsewhere, since word will spread quickly among investor networks.

❻ 'Innovators who seek to revolutionise and disrupt an industry must tell investors the truth about what their technology can do today – not just what they hope it might do some day.'

Jina Choi, Director of the US Securities and Exchange Commission's San Francisco Regional Office

What does due diligence involve?

You can think of due diligence as a qualifying process. Is the team as good as it says it is? Does the technology work or is it very likely to? Is there a demand for the technology? Do the financial projections make sense? Or you can think about it as the starting point in getting to know each other better, so that when things become more formal and legal documents are drawn up, both investors and entrepreneurs are confident that everyone involved is aligned. And don't forget – the entrepreneurs will be doing due diligence on you, too, since they'll be equally concerned that the best possible outcome is achieved.

Search on the internet, and you can find all sorts of variations on due diligence. There are brief summaries consisting of a few bullet points, and 400+ page documents outlining what you should do in minute detail.

Jurisdiction is a particular point to note when looking online. There are numerous angel groups in the US, some of them very large, and while the underlying principles of due diligence may be the same, some of the advice won't necessarily apply where you are, especially around tax relief and regulations. The advice may also be geared towards much larger numbers of investors than you are likely to work with, and be based on different definitions of, for instance, a high net worth individual. Make sure you take account of context before acting on anything you find online. As with all advice (including mine), take what you need and what works for you, and ignore what isn't relevant.

There are different levels of due diligence, and some of them happen in parallel. The first step is to look for relevant information in the public domain that supports what the entrepreneurs have put in their pitch deck and business plan. Once you're happy with that stage, you'll want to look at more detailed information, such as the company accounts (if there are any yet), any market research they have commissioned themselves, patent filings and other confidential information. We'll look at the paperwork in more depth in Chapter 6, but remember that these things will most likely be happening alongside each other.

Some entrepreneurs expect you to sign non-disclosure agreements, NDAs, before they'll hand over the information you need, because otherwise they fear you'll tell the world their brilliant idea. As I mentioned in the previous chapter, I'll only sign an NDA if it relates to proprietary technology, where the patents have not yet been filed. While an innovation cannot be patented if it is already described in the public domain (because it is no longer classed as novel), signing an NDA as a potential investor will not negate the patent application because that puts you on the inside. If the

entrepreneurs want you to sign NDAs to do with other company information, they may be subject to confidentiality agreements with other parties, they may be being over-cautious, or they may simply be ill-informed, and perhaps should seek external advice.

It's easier if you structure your due diligence as a series of investigations into different aspects of the business. Always start with the team, as if there are any doubts about them, you will be able to stop before putting in too much work. And don't forget to use your fellow investors, too – even if you're deal lead and expected to do most of the heavy lifting in due diligence, don't forget to call in co-investors for help if they have greater sector or subject expertise in a particular area.

Due diligence basics

The team
The technology
The defensibility
The market
The business
The finances

You can see that due diligence looks remarkably similar to my investment criteria – and that makes sense, because the due diligence process for me is about demonstrating how my investment criteria will translate into a viable business. Let's take a look at the individual elements of due diligence so you can start to build a picture of how you can translate your own investment criteria into a due diligence framework.

The team

I can't overstate how critical it is to back the right people, but how do you get from gut instinct to confidence?

> 'Early on [in my angel investing career] I'd fall in love with the idea, and not focus as much as I should have on the entrepreneur.'
>
> Meganne Houghton-Berry,
> UK Angel of the Year 2017

What kind of things are you looking for in an entrepreneur? I like to think that I back people who can walk through walls – they are passionate and driven and will do everything humanly possible to make their business succeed. But I also want to see that they are clear-eyed about their idea, and not so driven that they can't adapt if need be. Besides, some entrepreneurs are much quieter when you first meet them, and it might take a while to get to know their strengths. This is where due diligence comes in – and the first job is to find out if you were right about the team, before you start to dig more deeply into the business proposition itself.

We're all familiar with meeting someone new and taking an instant like – or dislike – to them. When you're talking about large sums of money that you might not see again, it's more comfortable to look at facts, numbers and market data than trust your gut. But start with your intuition and then look for the details that confirm – or refute – your first instincts. Chances are that if your intuition said 'no' from the get-go, then it will take an awful lot of hard evidence to convince yourself otherwise; but conversely, this could be a good thing, as it will give you extra confidence if you decide to move forward with the opportunity.

The easiest way to start finding out about the team is to go online. You'll almost certainly find your entrepreneurs on LinkedIn, where you can see whether they already have useful networks of connections, but do bear in mind that the only person who can edit a LinkedIn profile is the owner of that profile, so they can add, embellish and omit whatever they want. You can check if they have a public Facebook page or blog, look at their posts on Twitter or

Instagram, or check that their claim to be in a research group at a top university is accurate. In the UK, you might also want to check with Companies House to make sure that they are registered as directors, and when they came on board. I once had a rather strange email exchange with someone inviting me to invest in a company. Checking on Companies House revealed not only that they had been appointed director of the company several months before the founders, which didn't make sense, but also that there were some anomalies in the claims for sizes and rounds of investments. The Companies House records are based on government data, audited and very transparent, so I trusted them rather than what was in the emails, and was called 'barmy' for my trouble.

> I looked up the public Facebook page of a potential investee and found a picture of them wingsuit flying – which shows a great appetite for risk, but meant I had to have an important conversation with them about key man insurance.

You might want to think twice about an entrepreneur who turns out to have several different internet personalities – are they the serious tech geek of the blog, the corporate ninja portrayed on LinkedIn, or the keen adventurer who seems to have spent a lot of time sampling ayahuasca? Of course, all this might make them a very interesting person, but might cast doubts on their ability to concentrate on the business.

Can psychometric tests help when assessing the team? Headhunters and consultants like to use psychometric tools to see if a team will be a good fit, and it seems that some VCs are beginning to use these tests on entrepreneurs before investing. I'm not convinced this is a worthwhile exercise. A recent article in the *Financial Times* described how the British Antarctic Survey (BAS), which sends teams of people to spend months at a time in remote and inhospitable places, puts together its teams. It is vital that BAS gets this right – a bad team member could ruin a winter's work. They trialled psychometric testing over a period of six years to see if it could help in team selection. The results showed that a few of the tests were potentially useful, but that some team members who completed very successful postings in the Antarctic would have been rejected if the tests had been applied. This type of analysis can also be very expensive, so perhaps it's a cost worth avoiding.

You're hoping that your online searches will reveal not only that the team are who they say they are, but will also give you an idea of their entrepreneurial potential. This would most obviously include working at start-up companies or starting their own company, but they might have been entrepreneurial in other ways, for instance, as an academic they may have established and run a research group.

You may also get a sense of their attitude to learning, and whether they understand what they are lacking. Are they willing to listen to advice during due diligence, take it on board – or perhaps disagree convincingly and without being defensive? I have never seen a start-up team with the complete set of management skills to found, run and scale a business, so they will need to be receptive to advice about how to fill the gaps. The right attitude to learning could be crucial later on, if things start to go off track and you and your fellow investors feel you must intervene. Founders who refuse to listen and learn make trouble for everyone.

> ❝ 'If you listen to advice and say, "that doesn't apply to us", then you're not learning anything. The more you can learn from other people's experience, the more you save yourself from having to go through those experiences yourself. It's really important to listen to advice. If you can avoid making the same mistakes as other people, then why not?'
>
> Fiona Nielsen, co-founder of Repositive

You also want to get a feel for whether they have the passion and ability to inspire the team who will be working with them on this new venture, inspire confidence in other stakeholders, including you as an investor, and enthuse customers. If there are any, you might want to look at service contracts to see if the provisions for employees are consistent with the business goals.

Finally, do they understand that the CEO may not be leading the company in five years' time, or when it exits? Again, this is to do with their attitude to learning and willingness to listen, and their own self-awareness. Watching their reaction when you point this out can tell you a lot about them.

What you want in a team

- Passion
- Drive
- Transparency and honesty
- Awareness of their own limitations
- Willingness to learn
- Willingness to listen
- Balanced appetite for risk
- Ability to inspire

My investment criteria, particularly my technology focus and stipulation that companies should be within a certain distance from where I live, have influenced how I've picked teams to invest in. Looking at my portfolio data over the years, I can also see that I haven't always met my own two-founders rule, since the average size of the founding team is 1.8. The average age of the founders I have invested in is 38.4 years, and 45% were repeat entrepreneurs. A fifth of the founders I have invested in were born overseas, and only 7% were female. Fewer than 10% had MBAs but over 95% had degrees.

Some of these numbers reflect the fact that I invest in the technology sector in the UK – for instance, the proportion of women founders in UK B2B tech companies is low, although higher in the life sciences (which is a sector outside my criteria), and tech companies are more likely to be founded by graduates. I would like to see more women founding and leading tech companies. Plenty has been written about why the numbers are so low, and also why women are less likely to secure funding from VCs as they seek to grow their companies through later funding rounds. Having looked at my own numbers, I'll certainly be doing more in future to support women tech entrepreneurs where I can.

The technology

I have a technology background, so I mostly invest in companies that are developing a technology to bring to market, in sectors that I understand and am familiar with. Scaling a business is much easier with a technology product than providing a service, which only scales with the number of employees. Service businesses have exit valuations based on the number and retention of employees by the acquiring company, whereas product companies are based on the defensibility of the technology and their much easier ability to scale. These are reasons why I do not invest in service companies.

Having decided that the team is investable, I then need to know if the technology they are developing has promise. Will it work and will customers want to buy it?

A typical question people ask, though, is 'Is it disruptive?' What does that even mean? Lots of entrepreneurs claim that their technology is disruptive, but if it's just a better mousetrap, it will only ever be a better mousetrap. Sure, people may well want to buy a better mousetrap, but then you're simply stuck in the mousetrap business with nowhere else to go.

Something truly disruptive breaks the mould but by its very nature is hard to spot. With disruptive technologies, you can never say, 'I'll know it when I see it', because there are so many external factors involved, never mind whether the technology actually works. Simon King, of Octopus Ventures, told me about an investment in a technology for hailing taxis in London a few years ago. Their competitor research threw up a little company in the US called UberCab, but there were no data on how successful it was, the company hadn't had much significant funding, and it was concentrating on private hire cars in the Bay Area, so Simon and his colleagues figured it wasn't much of a threat. Then Google Ventures stepped in with a $258 million investment in what was by now called Uber, which kickstarted the company's international expansion and the rest, as they say, made Octopus Ventures' investment history.

Disruptive technology is only obvious after the fact. Luckily, due diligence on the technology is about far more concrete things than whether or not the entrepreneurs' misty-eyed vision of a disrupted future might come true.

But ultimately, is it ready? Are the founders presenting you with a fully developed new technology that is ready to be marketed, or are they still in the development process? Have they even got past proof of concept? Each of these stages will require different levels of investment and different types of expertise. You need to understand the situation fully so that you can judge whether you think the founders are capable of taking their technology to the next stage, whatever that may be.

The defensibility

What must be defensible? Coca-Cola's secret formula is a marketing gimmick, not a defensible technology. But the Coca-Cola brand is highly defensible, and is what makes it so hard for another company to break into the cola drink market.

There's no point in founding a company to market a technology that anyone else can copy. If it can't be patented or protected in some other way, what are the reasons and can they be overcome? If it can be patented, will it have to be patented in different territories, with all the additional administration and costs that will entail?

And even if a start-up has had a patent granted, will be it able to defend that patent against the might of a large company. It is said that it can cost £5 million to defend a patent, which of course, may be unsuccessful.

In my view, having 'freedom to operate' (FTO) is much more important than a patent. In other words, will the start-up tread on the toes of another company, leading to an expensive court case, a lengthy product redesign or a profit-reducing licence deal?

Defensibility is forward-looking, but should at least be at the back of everyone's minds from the early stages. This can be as basic as the company's name. Does it do what it says on the tin? I've seen numerous examples of technology companies that have changed their names as they've evolved, to describe more clearly what they do or to make it easier for them to offer additional products. The rapidly growing Cambridge Medical Robotics recently re-branded as CMR Surgical, a name that the company believes better reflects its ambitious vision, whereas True Knowledge re-branded as Evi, the name of its voice interface, when Evi started to gain traction in the market.

Defensibility is not just about the brand. It could also be about speed to market – the first to gain traction with customers can secure a commanding position.

The market

A pitch deck must include a certain amount of market research, but all too often the founders will claim to be selling into a huge market so there's lots of potential. For instance, they may be targeting the mobile phone market, and since there are reported to be over 4.5 billion mobile phone users on the planet, they only need to capture 0.01% of it to be looking at big sales figures.

This is a classic example of the top down/bottom up problem in analysing the market. Yes, there are a lot of mobile phone users in the world, but why on earth would they want to buy this particular product? What do the customers, the end users, actually need, or want? Just because there are billions of them does not mean they will automatically buy the product.

So in the pitch deck, I look for the founders' understanding of the potential market, but also an understanding of their customer and the assumptions they have made to come up with their projected figures. Are the numbers robust, do they make sense, are they justified?

I do look for evidence of a large market. If it is a very niche product, it may only have a small, niche market – which won't generate fantastic returns for the investors. Here is where sticking to what you know is an advantage – I know and understand B2B, so I will already have some idea of the market across several sectors.

I also look for evidence that the founders understand where their product fits in the value chain, because that will affect not only sales channels but also pricing and profitability. The higher up the value chain, that is, the nearer the end customer, the greater the profits will be. The coffee mug in my hand started as clay in the ground, and went through a number of stages to reach my kitchen table. The clay producer sold a batch of clay to the manufacturer, the manufacturer made the mug and sold it to the wholesaler, the wholesaler sold the mug to the retailer, and I went to the shop and bought it. The price of the clay could have been less than 1,000th of the price I paid.

Have your entrepreneurs identified who their customer is, their user and their buyer? These might be three different people – for instance, if the technology is a new camera for mobile phones, the user will be the person who chooses to buy that mobile phone, but the entrepreneur will not be selling to them. They may not even be selling to the designers in the mobile phone company, but to a contracted manufacturer (most probably in the Far East).

Identifying the buyer is a start but then the entrepreneur has to be able to get to them. Are there suitable channels in place? How will the entrepreneur access those channels, and how will they tackle the competition? Do they know who and where the competition is? You will expect the business plan to have identified the buyers and also ways to sell to them.

What if there is no obvious market but the entrepreneurs are convinced they can create one? They, and you, will have to work much harder to decide if the technology really does meet a need, and creating a new market will require particular skills and a considerably higher sales and marketing budgets. Angels are not keen on funding the surprisingly large and undefined costs of creating a new market and the cost and time of educating customers.

The business

> 'The responsibility to become "a scale-up nation" – to create an environment (ecosystem) where a greater number of companies reach global scale – rests with all of us who have an interest in supporting economic growth.'
>
> Sherry Coutu, *The Scale-Up Report on UK Economic Growth*

What I look for is a business that can scale. I want an opportunity with a sustainable business model, a realistic go-to-market plan, a deep marketing strategy and a future product and technology pipeline. But realistically, investors are never presented with a perfect business plan at the first pitch. Due diligence will help you to refine what is presented, and create a business plan with the founders that makes sense, has believable assumptions and is, hopefully, achievable.

A lot of what you will be doing at this point will be feeding into the term sheet, as you will be negotiating ownership of the business, articles of association and valuation, and generally understanding how efficiently the business has been set up and whether it is being run professionally.

You also want to know when the entrepreneurs see the business becoming profitable, as that will be a major milestone towards exit. The fundamental fact of life is that any company needs money from somewhere to survive. Grants cannot run a company for long, and sufficient debt is rarely available for a rapidly scaling business, so it is down to equity from investors and of course, cash from customers.

Generally, the goal is for investors to keep funding a company until it reaches breakeven, that is, starts to fund itself through sales (rather than investment, debt or grants) or exit. But research shows that 75% of all start-ups are shut down by the investors because they no longer believe in the founders, before the company reaches breakeven or exit.

Shareholders cannot continue to follow on with more funding forever and loans are only temporary; they will have to be paid back at some point. If any potential exit is too far in the future, can you really wait? Remember that you shouldn't be expecting a return on your investment for eight to ten years, but nor should you be prepared to hang on for 15 or 20 years. Mind you, on the US West Coast, profitability is often a low priority because investors there are more comfortable with the unknown. They will invest in businesses where profitability, indeed how the idea will be monetised at all, is really not obvious at the outset. A cultural hangover from the dotcom boom perhaps, and only a few have got lucky – Twitter recorded around $2.5 billion in losses over 11 years until it finally announced a profitable quarter in late 2017.

Growth potential is another key element to explore. If the entrepreneurs have fully explored the market for their technology, they may see a rapidly expanding opportunity. So then the question is whether they have used this information to develop a strategy to cope with rapid growth and fast-expanding sales – can they scale?

The finances

What do the entrepreneurs want to do with your money? Is there a clear plan to spend it on proof of concept, product development, hiring key executives, building a sales team, or marketing activities in specific sectors or geographies? If the team haven't decided what they intend to use the money for, then they haven't yet got a well-considered business plan. If you're impressed with the team, this could be something that you might want to help them develop, but you must at least feel that they have some idea of what will be needed to create a successful business.

But before you start to look at what might happen post-investment, you want to be sure that the entrepreneurs are good at managing the money they have already raised, or earned through sales. You need to reassure yourself that all the financial transactions are compliant, tax returns and accounts are being filed and, at a later stage, professional auditors have reviewed the accounts. Along with that, you'll review whether the company has applied for EIS tax relief, if eligible, and also if it is registered for VAT.

Finance factors to look for include:
- Realistic gross margins, calculated correctly
- Realistic channel costs
- Price erosion/cost increases considered
- Risks in existing commercial agreements evaluated
- Presence of exclusivities
- Clean investment structure with alignment of interests
- Debt
- Recruitment budget
- IP protection and progression budget

The company will probably have been formed, and ownership between founders agreed, but the types of companies I invest in are unlikely to have started trading or have any accounts to review. Some angels prefer to invest a bit later in the life of a company, when they have more information to go on, and customers.

No time for regrets

You do your due diligence and something doesn't feel quite right, so you pass up the opportunity to invest. No problem, you've got another 20 business plans in your inbox to wade through, and you know you'll bring more value to the right one. But then that opportunity you turned down becomes Google, Amazon, SwiftKey. I could have invested in the last one but a combination of factors prevented me, including the fact that the syndicate I was following fizzled out.

But do I regret it? Well, it would have been nice to have that cheque when Microsoft stepped in and bought the company (which we'll talk more about when we talk about exits) but I'm just one of millions of investors who said no to an investment for all sorts of valid reasons that were ultimately proved wrong.

Or were we wrong? Remember my investment criteria? They've been developed over years and have stood the test of time. I can't be constantly looking for the outlier because outliers by definition don't fit what you have pictured in your head. I know full well that VC funds expect only one in ten of their investments to make it to the big time, and most to fail, so if I went around regretting things, I'd have no energy left to nurture the companies in my portfolio.

> One company I did turn down was into hydroponics. They said the technology was being used to grow tomatoes but it smelled of cannabis to me – and it was outside my 90-minute rule – so I said no. It turned out to be a good business, and I could have made a reasonable return, but I turned it down for the right reasons.

People increasingly talk about FOMO – the fear of missing out – but that way madness lies. Just look at the numbers. I get more than 1,000 business plans a year, I reject 95% outright, I start due diligence on 5%, and actively investigate 2%. Eventually, I might invest in eight to ten companies, or 1%. What if the 1,000 or so I've turned down all turned out to be winners? Well, then I'd stop being an angel investor – but they don't. So regretting the minuscule proportion that I reject but turn out well is a mug's game.

> I hope by now it's clear that invested investors work with a lot of people, not only the founding teams of the companies they invest in, but also fellow investors who put in money alongside them and share the burden and ultimately the spoils, if things go according to plan. Time to take a closer look at what co-investing involves.

INVESTED INVESTOR TAKEAWAY

● Be open with your entrepreneurs about how you will conduct due diligence, the topics to be covered and what you find as you proceed.
● Look at the team first; if it's the wrong team, don't invest.
● If the opportunity is in tech, identify if the product is ready for market or still in development.
● Investigate the defensibility of the business idea or product.
● Make sure that market expectations are realistic.
● Look for a sustainable business model.
● Be confident about the finances and plans for how the investment will be spent.
● Don't waste time regretting the ones that got away.

AN INVESTOR'S STORY:
My due diligence surprises

Even with the most careful attention to detail, there's always something you might miss – and there's always the chance the founders will throw a curve ball at the most unexpected time. Over the years, there have been a few occasions when my due diligence has been stopped in its tracks by a remark from one of the team.

One founder called me to say he was firing one of his co-founders, who happened to be the CTO. Luckily that happened before the investment closed, so we weren't suddenly investing in a different team without the technology whizzkid the business was supposedly being built around.

Another time, one of the two founders came to a fellow angel and said, 'I want my own office'. Some of us might find that reasonable, but when you're investing in a team of two co-founders, and one is separating themselves from the other, that's a sure sign that they're no longer getting on and things are going to fall apart pretty soon, which did happen.

Yet another painful lesson was when the team decided they didn't want our money. I and my co-investors had put in a lot of work mentoring them, going through the details of the business plan, helping them to get investment ready and building a round. They turned us away without so much as a thank you. The company is growing very slowly as a result of their decision to bootstrap rather than take investment, when it could have been a different story – although ultimately perhaps better for the founders if the company succeeds. Not all companies benefit from external investment, and bootstrapping means the founders keep 100% of the ownership – but conversely, without external investment they won't get the help of other, more experienced entrepreneurs. Advisors can be brought in as non-shareholding directors or on consultancy arrangements when needed, but they won't be as invested in the business as an angel funder will be.

Finally, a technology surprise. On a conference call where my fellow investors and the founders were discussing their proposed business, one of the investors pointed out that he had found a patent in the US that could cause serious problems. The founding team knew about the patent but didn't think that their technology was competing so hadn't bothered to tell us about it. That inevitably raised questions in our minds about what else they might be keeping from us, whether in the mistaken opinion that it wasn't important or, more seriously, because they were trying to conceal information. Could we trust them? The funding round collapsed.

CHAPTER 5

Co-investing

C o-investing is essential. As an invested investor, you need to be selective about who you invest with, not only because you need to feel confident that they'll stick with the company and follow on when further investment is needed as the founders get their venture off the ground, but also because you will be working closely with them on helping the company to succeed. Entrepreneurs, too, need to be choosy about their investors – there's nothing worse than an entrepreneur taking an investment out of desperation for the money and then finding that it's toxic, coming with too much interference and too many strings attached.

All money is not the same

'I turned down the opportunity to do business with a guy who opened his briefcase to reveal that it contained £30,000 in cash, and a gun.'

Richard Lucas, entrepreneur
and investor based in Poland

People talk about dumb money and smart money, but I don't think those classifications tell the whole story.

Dumb money is really passive money – where the investor simply puts up the cash and has neither the interest, nor the time, nor perhaps the ability to help the company grow and succeed. The whole point of being an invested investor is to use your skills to help build companies, provide employment, provide what customers need and hopefully change the world. If you just write a cheque and sit back, your talents will be wasted and you won't have nearly so much fun – mind you, you might not have nearly so much stress, either.

Some passive money is actually more what I'd call passive-aggressive money. For instance, I've read that around 20% of angel investors in one European country refuse to co-invest. I assume this is because they don't want interference from other investors, or simply think they're on to a winner and want to keep it all to themselves. An entrepreneur feeling that their investor has put all their eggs in one basket – and that basket happens to be them – might feel another level of stress and, quite frankly, extra stress is the last thing an entrepreneur needs.

Even the money you might invest as a family member or friend of the entrepreneur carries risks. Your motives won't necessarily be purely objective, and sometimes your judgement can be clouded, so don't be offended if the entrepreneur is a bit cautious about taking your well-intended offer. There are cases where family and friends invest because they want a role in the company, and we all know families that have problems with Christmas, let alone those who are trying to run a fast-growing and stressful start-up.

I'm not totally opposed to the family and friends model but it has limitations. Family and friends money brings its own obligations and responsibilities, not least because it might be someone's savings, or their rainy day money, and intended as a purchase of equity that is expected to be repaid eventually rather than an outright gift. These investors are also much less likely to do the kind of due diligence that might shed light on issues that need to be addressed before they become detrimental to the company. From my experience, family and friends are particularly insensitive on valuation (wanting their relative or friend to keep as much of the company as possible), meaning that later rounds may be a down-round, where the valuation is lower than the preceding round and the dilution therefore greater, which is painful for all. That said, one UK survey estimated that some 1.6 million individuals had invested over £776 million in start-ups as family and friends between 2014 and 2016, so it plays an important role in this ecosystem.

I always tell the entrepreneurs I meet not to take money from just one person or source, so co-investing is a given for me. A group of external investors may require more managing, on both sides, but is much more useful to the entrepreneurs – and they are much more useful to each other. Having a group of investors opens up more than one network, means there is more cash available (as long as all investors understand the likelihood of needing to follow on and are prepared to do so) and a greater range of knowledge and experience. That knowledge and experience will include not only familiarity with the sector and connections to key individuals, potential colleagues and potential customers, but also knowledge of how to do due diligence and some of the specialisms, such as legal and financial, that will underpin the deal.

So as a new angel, you should be looking out for positive, proactive fellow investors to work alongside as you develop your own knowledge of investing in and building new companies.

The relationship changes once the cheques have cleared. Originally, the entrepreneurs are selling shares in their business and the angels are buying them, so it's a sales exercise, with the angels gathering information as part of due diligence, and the entrepreneurs providing what they want to share that they hope will close the deal. When both sides are comfortable with both the information and the working relationship that has developed, the legal documents are drawn up, the round closes and the money is transferred – and then the entrepreneur must start to deliver.

When there are different investor groups offering all the money, the entrepreneur has to choose between them and things are slightly different. In this situation, you may essentially get an auction, where the investors each try to persuade the entrepreneur that they are the best option. This is, of course, good for the entrepreneur, because they have started a bidding war and that usually pushes prices up. Now, the investors are trying to sell their cash and the entrepreneur is deciding whose cash to accept, that is, the roles have switched. That being said, there are many examples of entrepreneurs negotiating common terms and raising money from both groups.

But bidding wars can be divisive and the entrepreneur wants more than one investor. This is where it becomes important to understand how co-investors can work together.

ENTREPRENEUR TAKEAWAY

While potential investors are doing due diligence on you and your co-founders, you should be doing your own due diligence on them.

Be careful who you invest with

In all walks of life, there are some people you might find incredibly difficult to work with, for all kinds of reasons. Investors are no different – just as you're careful selecting which entrepreneurs you feel comfortable and confident about working with, you have to be equally selective about who you choose as co-investors.

It's almost certainly going to be a challenging journey, and people can act in unexpected ways when there's money involved. So watch out for potential co-investors who show signs of being difficult. You may have to take time to decide whether or not they will add sufficient value to outweigh any problems in working together.

In the early stages, some investors may spend inordinate amounts of time with the entrepreneurs, asking questions that may not be pertinent for the company at its present stage, requesting yet more data about markets and potential customers, and generally poking into everything they can think of. I find City types are often the worst for this, as they've come from a rarefied world of big deals, with big groups of research staff doing all the background checks for them.

Frustratingly, sometimes the investor who spends the most time on the preliminaries only invests a small amount in the first round (if at all) and doesn't follow on. In some cases, I suspect that the time spent asking for more information and going over every detail with a fine-toothed comb is actually because they are scared of investing, so it's not surprising when they only put in a modest sum and drop out early.

So another part of the co-investing story is for all the investors to be open about how much money they are willing to put in, and to be willing to cooperate and co-ordinate due diligence activity.

Investors with small shareholdings from the first round can also complicate things at exit if the legal documentation hasn't allowed for this and specified how many shares must be voted to agree an exit. If nothing is agreed, which is unlikely, someone holding 1% or even less can cause problems – something we'll cover in more detail in the next chapter when we look at shareholder rights.

Then there's the question of time wasting. Investors who want to know everything in exhaustive detail could end up slowing the growth of the company if they keep insisting on being kept up to date with everything that is going on. If you're the lead investor and have a seat on the Board, you may be able to manage this, but be aware that it could be an issue.

How many co-investors do you need?

I advocate investing alongside other angels. It spreads the risk and brings diverse skills and expertise to the table – complementing your own experience and giving the founders that extra chance of success. I always co-invest.

Co-investing means investing along with a group of other investors in the same round. You can do this most easily with crowdfunding, but that won't make you an invested investor. Nevertheless, I do advocate considering starting your angel investing journey this way, just to dip your toes in the water. You will probably be investing alongside a lot of other people but your goal in crowdfunding is simply to learn, from comparing pitch decks, analysing teams, following chat forums about particular opportunities and generally getting to know the terminology.

Once you're ready to start investing with a smaller angel group or syndicate, you need to be aware of the benefits of co-investing and potential pitfalls. So how many co-investors are the right number for you and for the company?

It's partly about the round. Different stages in the lifecycle of a company require not only different levels of input from investors but also different amounts of money – from the thousands of the early rounds to potentially millions in later rounds.

In the very beginning, there should be at least three or four investors, chosen carefully. Once you've made a few investments, your network will start to expand and you'll have a pool of potential co-investors you can approach so you can select the right people for the particular opportunity.

You should expect entrepreneurs to be very wary of taking all the money they need from a single investor for all sorts of reasons. A single investor means a single large shareholder, alongside the founders, which has implications for control and strategy, as well as later rounds. Imagine if there is a single investor and that investor does not follow on when cash is needed. What are new investors going to think? Two investors are slightly better but I'd argue that's still too few to bring the right amount of diversity of experience to the table.

Conversely, you don't want too many investors. I've seen first rounds of 20 investors, which starts to get unwieldy, and even 30. It's hard enough managing a few co-investors, but when there are so many, it can be very difficult to obtain consensus when there are tricky decisions to be made. A nominee structure would ease that process but someone probably needs to pay for that. A caveat to that is the life sciences sector, where start-ups typically need a lot more money and a lot more time to prove their technology and gain the necessary regulatory approval, and so may well need a larger number of early investors.

Over time, the company should be looking for bigger tranches of money as it grows and the goal is to secure fewer investors with bigger pockets. A few large cheques are better than many small ones; shareholdings are less complex and there are fewer investors for the lead investors or entrepreneurs to manage. By this point, you're likely to stop following on by investing in later rounds.

> If the valuation of one of my companies exceeds, say, £10 million, I very rarely follow on. Because of the financial and valuation limits I have set myself as an angel investor, my follow-on investment would be too small a proportion of the overall

company. It's of little benefit to the company to have me investing, say, £20,000, when others are putting in £2 million. My 1% contribution is a drop in the ocean at this point. I'm not selling out, just stopping, because I know where my money and expertise could be better used – and that is in helping other start-ups and small companies. Once one of my investments is looking at valuations in the millions, I know it needs different types of expertise from different types of investor.

Another benefit of co-investors is that they can keep you in the loop when you're not closely involved with one of your companies. If I worked 24/7, I still couldn't give all the companies in my portfolio all the attention they might need – and I'd have to kiss my family and social life goodbye. Like everyone else, investors have to prioritise their time, and having a group of co-investors that you trust and can rely on makes it possible to build a portfolio with confidence. Even if I'm not actively involved in one of my portfolio companies, my co-investors know I will respond if either they or the entrepreneurs involved ask for help or advice. It's a question of teamwork. For some investments, I'm leading the deal and then becoming investor director and highly proactive; for others I'm taking a backseat role but ready to help if needed. There are times when I feel a bit guilty that I'm not helping more, but that is why I don't invest alone, and you shouldn't – there'll always be a time when you need to spread the load.

Co-investing means someone has to lead the deal

Efficient angel investing requires one of the investors to lead the deal, to take charge of ensuring that due diligence is completed, ensure that all the legal paperwork is in place and the money pledged and accounted for. They have to be willing to put in a lot of time and effort – they're the most invested investor, if you like. In fact, any invested investor should either be deal lead at least once, or be willing to be a deal lead if necessary, that is, they should have the skills and understanding to fulfil the role. I have been deal lead on more than 20 rounds, and most invested investors will have led – or been willing to lead – rounds in several companies.

It is crucial to understand that, in the UK, the deal lead doesn't have any legal or moral responsibility to their fellow investors. Even though deal leading could be thought of as effectively equivalent to a Financial Conduct Authority (FCA) regulated role, because the deal lead is ultimately promoting an investment, a group of angel investors is an unregulated entity and each investor is self-certified as a high net worth individual and/or a sophisticated investor, so ultimately the decision to invest is theirs and theirs alone.

> Invested investors understand that, even when they invest with others, they are making an independent decision about how to invest their own money.

Never be a deal lead the first time you invest in a start-up; you have too much to learn and there are too many aspects of the road to exit that you don't yet understand. I mentioned City types and their desire for information earlier – and they may be the exception to the rule here. Their experience might make them ready to operate as deal lead earlier as they have relevant skills, but don't take that for granted and make sure you are comfortable with them in the role.

Others should go slowly at first and learn the ropes. Deal leading is very time-consuming (it has been likened to herding cats), and if you're seeking to get enough deals done to build your portfolio in the early stages, you won't have time to act as deal lead for a while, anyway.

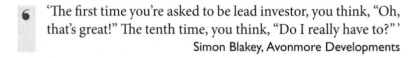

> 'The first time you're asked to be lead investor, you think, "Oh, that's great!" The tenth time, you think, "Do I really have to?"'
> Simon Blakey, Avonmore Developments

Some angel groups have a buddying system, a bit like shadowing someone in their job. New investors can observe the process and learn what it means to lead a deal before they take the plunge. Buddies can also keep an eye on the process, making sure you don't miss any steps out along the way. Similarly, other angel groups include new investors as 'interns' during due diligence, provide or recommend courses to take, or don't let new angels invest during the first year. Personally, I think the last two approaches are wrong. I don't believe the classroom is the right place to learn about investing, and I've said elsewhere that taking the plunge is critical to gaining experience and starting to build up a portfolio – that can't be achieved if you're expected to stand by and watch for a year.

Deal leading, if done properly, implies a lot of work, including large amounts of research, administration and project management. Among their many tasks, the deal lead must discover and potentially negotiate how much each individual angel will pledge, and act as the central point for the process of putting together term sheets, shareholder agreements and other legal requirements. They will also end up doing a lot of the research involved in due diligence, and have to make sure all the information pertinent to the deal reaches all the potential investors. They have to convene meetings and conduct negotiations as things draw towards the close, and ensure that everyone involved understands the negotiations and is able to make a fully informed decision.

You may not be the sole deal lead, particularly when it's a very complex deal or there are very large sums of money involved. Cambridge Angels have collaborated successfully as co-leads with 24 Haymarket and Cambridge Capital Group, among others, on several occasions. If you make your first investments through crowdfunding platforms, then it is often the entrepreneur who acts as deal lead and should provide you with all the due diligence and other relevant information. It's different for the equity funding platform Syndicate Room, where each deal has to be proposed and led by an experienced angel or angel group.

Once the deal is closed, the lead's job doesn't end there. When I'm leading a deal, I make sure the legal documents include criteria for how the investors are kept up to date with information from the company, and I keep an eye on how this is going, as some entrepreneurs are better at updating their investors than others. I also make ad hoc announcements to investors if I become aware that the founders need particular technical expertise or introductions to potential customers.

Although it's no longer a legal requirement in the UK, I also recommend an annual meeting similar to an AGM. This is a good opportunity for everyone to come together, and allows the entrepreneur or founders to re-sell their business and vision to the investors, prepare the ground for subsequent funding rounds, describe what help they need and ask for contacts. An annual meeting for shareholders not only strengthens the connections between the entrepreneurs and their investors, it also helps to build networks and encourages investors to become more active if they aren't already helping the company to the best of their ability. There are also implications for the exit – companies that are acquisition targets benefit from demonstrating that they have been run professionally, and some form of annual shareholder meeting is a part of that process.

Just occasionally, the deal lead may have to reject one of the potential investors before the deal closes. If they and the other investors feel that the relationship isn't going to work, or the potential rogue investor is proving to be more of a hindrance than a help to the enterprise (perhaps mentioning EIS too often, suggesting they're only interested in the tax relief), it could be down to the deal lead to remove them from the equation. Again, this is where considered decisions based on valid evidence are required. I've done this several times for a variety of reasons, the most difficult being a relative of one of the founders, who had a private equity background and wanted multi-year founder vesting terms that I thought were unnecessarily strict.

What if the entrepreneur is the deal lead?

There are occasions where the entrepreneur ends up fulfilling the role of deal lead. It's definitely a situation of *caveat emptor*, as the entrepreneur may over-sell the deal.

You may find the entrepreneur has to act as deal lead because no one else is willing to take it on (in which case, think very hard about your fellow investors). Or it may simply be because the entrepreneur wants to be deal lead. Experienced entrepreneurs who have had successful exits in the past and are investing their own money alongside the angels are more likely to want to act as deal lead.

Another situation where the entrepreneur might end up as deal lead is when the rounds are allowed to drag on for a long time – but this is not a good situation to be in. In my view, investment rounds need hard closing dates, otherwise they can take up too much of everybody's time, time that could be better spent on finding customers and growing the business. There's also the risk that not enough money is raised to implement the plan that the founders proposed when the round opened.

You need to make sure you understand the reasons and motives behind an entrepreneur being deal lead rather than one of the investors, and make sure that you are comfortable with that scenario before you invest.

Valuations

A key role for the deal lead is to secure agreement on the valuation.

Valuations are based on tangible and intangible factors and can be very difficult to assess, particularly when the company is a start-up and much of the information used for the valuation is based on projections rather than historical data. If only valuing a company were as simple as buying a house in some countries, where the price is generally per square metre, and not based on subjective factors such as the proximity of a good school.

It is also the case that entrepreneurs are more savvy about valuations today than they were ten years ago – which is a good thing, but can also make negotiations more complex. Entrepreneurs have access to a lot of information on valuations through their networks or by being involved in accelerator programmes, and of course there is plenty of information available on the internet; they may get rather inflated ideas about how much their company is worth.

So you have to find some baseline criteria to begin with, such as looking at the valuations of similar-sized companies in the same or comparable sectors. You can also look at others in the same accelerator programme, if applicable, or recent start-ups in the same field. These data will help you come up with an initial number but there will inevitably be negotiations to follow (if this isn't a crowdfunded investment, where the valuation is set at the outset, generally by the entrepreneur).

Angels almost always think the entrepreneur is valuing the company too highly – which means angels get a smaller percentage of the company for their money – and don't factor in risk. New entrepreneurs in particular may have unrealistic ideas about what their company is worth and how quickly it will grow when it has no track record. Evidence from a number of areas, such as other companies and deals, future rounds and expected valuations, market potential and routes to market should help to bring them back to earth and allow both sides to come up with a reasonable figure.

There are occasions where everyone involved thinks that the valuation is fair and accepts it very quickly, which makes life a lot easier for all concerned.

Very rarely, a valuation might be negotiated up. I did that for one company, where the original valuation and the higher than expected availability of capital meant that the founders would have been left with too small a shareholding in their own company. If the founding team is not the major shareholder by a sufficient margin, they may be demotivated and everyone involved suffers as a result, particularly when dilution occurs at a later stage.

Valuations can get more complicated if a VC is involved and puts in a different term sheet to that of the angels, or angel group. There may be room for negotiation but some VCs and some angel groups have standard term sheets that they don't like to vary much. Until relatively recently, VCs didn't tend to get involved until later rounds, where the valuation is based on more concrete data than for the very earliest investments because the company has been operating for a while. Now that some VCs are getting into companies at the very early stages, it is even more important to stipulate that the original investors have first refusal at subsequent rounds – the pre-emption rule, or first option to buy – to avoid early dilution. If they have enough to invest, they may be able to prevent newcomers from getting into the round. However, incoming investors do bring new skills and connections, which are often valuable.

In all this, don't forget how important it is for the entrepreneurs to understand the different classes of share and the implications for an eventual exit – which is something you'll make sure of in the legal documents that define the size and extent of the investment by all parties involved.

Different classes of share are most likely to come into play in later rounds, when more money is needed and the company is more likely to be approaching VCs. In the past, VC investors rarely came in on the same share terms as the original angel investors and this is one of the reasons that led to VCs becoming known as 'vulture capitalists'. Nowadays, things are generally more aligned, with VCs more often coming in close to the same share terms as angels and founders. This makes working together far more pleasant and any future exit more equitable.

The valuation is also an important part of building trust at the beginning of the entrepreneurial journey. If it's going to be a long relationship – and that is usually the case – then all sides must agree that the valuation is fair, especially if there are both VC and angel investors and different classes of share. The deal lead has their work cut out.

> **TRANSPARENCY TAKEAWAY**
> Fair valuations provide a strong foundation.
> Being transparent in negotiations, and making sure all
> surrounding issues are heard and dealt with fairly, is critical for
> building trust going forward.

How do you choose who's going to lead the deal?

The deal lead is going to have to put in a lot of work and time both before and after the deal is done, since they should also expect to be on the Board, so you and your fellow investors need to be realistic when deciding between you who is going to take on the task.

Some angel groups have a formal system for choosing the deal lead. Among its investment criteria, the Cambridge Angels specify that the entrepreneurs have to be sponsored by one of the members in order to be introduced to the group's formal pitching process. The Cambridge Angel who brings the founders to the group is already enthusiastic about the proposition, will have carried out a certain amount of due diligence to get to this point and believe that the idea has potential, so they almost always become the deal lead by default.

Deal leads are not normally chosen systematically. A group of investors won't operate on an it's-your-turn basis; rather, the person best suited to be the deal lead in each instance typically volunteers. If no one offers to be deal lead, the group won't invest together, although some may invest independently. Alternatively, if no one in the group wants to lead the deal, another investor might be brought in specifically for this purpose, rather than to join the group for the long term.

The deal lead needs to be someone who can work well with the founders and their fellow investors, will be professional about the tasks that have to be completed and keep everyone on track to close the deal. It is usually bad for the entrepreneur, and for the investors, if the process drags on too long. Doing a deal too quickly can also be problematic. Trust and relationships need time to develop, and nobody wants what a fellow angel dubs the first 'Oh shit' moment to be in the first Board meeting post investment.

The challenges of co-investing

I've mentioned before that you must keep money in reserve for each investment so that you are able to follow on when your portfolio companies inevitably need more funding than originally envisaged to hit their milestones. When you're co-investing, I feel that there is a moral obligation not only to continue to support the entrepreneur but also to continue to support your fellow investors wherever possible.

Every investment is a personal decision but if you are a large investor and drop out of the second round, that could kill the deal and the company, and mean that everyone loses their money. I would suggest that your confidence in the team and the business has to drop a significant amount to prevent you from following on. I feel particularly obligated to invest in the second round when I'm the deal lead, as failing to follow on would almost certainly be the worst signal I could send about the state of the company.

If the co-investing group is large, someone dropping out might not be so much of a problem, as one or more of the other investors might be able to plug the gap. But when someone drops out so early, it may spook the others. Here's where transparency can be useful – if you have to drop out because of something unrelated to the company and the money (for instance, family illness), it is only fair to let your fellow investors know your reasons. Otherwise, they will be making their own decisions based on hearsay or their imagination, rather than concrete information.

> **TRANSPARENCY TAKEAWAY**
> Keep your co-investors informed if circumstances change. Don't let rumours and guesswork affect your co-investors' decisions. If you have to drop out, be honest about the reasons.

The Angel CoFund

One of the additional benefits of co-investing in the UK is the potential for additional investment from the Angel CoFund. I have not only been able to take advantage of co-funding for several of my portfolio companies, but have also been on the investment committee of the Angel CoFund for some years.

This government-backed fund invests alongside angel syndicates, matching the funding they are putting in up to a maximum of £1 million. The focus is on companies with high growth potential and, not surprisingly, there is a stringent set of criteria that have to be followed to secure investment, including extensive checks for money laundering and other abuses. One of the key points is that the Angel CoFund will only join a round with new investors; it won't invest where only existing investors are putting in a new round. This is for purely pragmatic reasons – new investors are more likely to do a thorough job of due diligence, whereas previous investors will think they already know enough about the company to skip some of this.

Money from the Angel CoFund is relatively passive but being able to raise a much larger sum than from angels alone can be a major boost. By its fifth anniversary in 2017, the Angel CoFund had invested a total of £32 million in 70 companies.

When it's time to go to the next level, what will a VC look for?

> 'VC money is like adding rocket fuel to a business. You can't leave the atmosphere without it, but then you can't slow down – or stop. And if the next injection of fuel isn't available, you'll crash.'
>
> Simon King, Octopus Ventures

If it's time to bring in VC money, then you need to know how a VC thinks in order to help your founders attract them and secure the investment.

I may be stating the obvious, but investing is what VCs do, 24/7 in some cases, whereas you as an angel might still be working or have other calls on your time so cannot devote the same number of hours to due diligence and everything else that investing involves. VCs also share the load because they're a mainly full-time, professional team, whereas you might be one of a group of angels with a deal lead who is as busy as you are, and will have to trust and rely on them when it comes to making a decision.

What do VCs look for? They look for stars. They know full well the odds of picking a winner are slim, but every company they choose to invest in must have the potential to return many multiples. Out of ten investments, the rule of thumb for VCs is typically that five will fail, three or four will do ok, and they hope that one will produce a return equal to the entire fund.

If none of the businesses in a VC portfolio fails, then they know they're not doing their job properly. Finding the companies that return many multiples means taking risks and if there are no failures, then they're not taking big enough risks and will never find the big successes. So a VC wants to invest in a business that has the potential to be worth, say, £500 million at exit. Whereas you, as an invested angel investor, can get a stellar return with a much smaller exit value.

Remember to keep things in perspective – the multiple matters. VCs want big returns because they are big investors – half a million might be a small sum to them, but a very large sum to an angel who has put in a few thousand at the beginning. It's the relative amount that is important to you as an invested investor, not the absolute amount. I like the description of exits as car-changing, house-changing or life-changing. I have already achieved two of those categories, and live in hope for the third.

VCs also see a lot more deals than angels, partly because they're geared up to it. One VC group I know gets around 3,000 business plans each year, and they meet between 300 and 500 of those companies. They have a dedicated new business team (again, they've got the time and the resources, whereas an angel/earlier stage investor doesn't), which will conduct all the due diligence and then make recommendations to the investment committee. Ultimately, out of those 3,000 plans, 15–20 will secure an investment.

Finally, the VCs will generally be coming in at a later stage, so there will be more information on customers, revenues, operating profit, etc., and a better chance of coming up with a realistic valuation of the company.

What can you do to improve the chances of your company attracting VC funding? Not very much if you're not on the Board or in frequent contact advising the founders. If you haven't built a strong mentoring relationship, they're not likely to come to you for advice and recommendations. But if you have built a good rapport, you may be able to help.

VCs will have their own criteria for assessing potential investments, many of which will look similar to yours, and some of which will reflect the fact that the company is at a later stage.

So what are VCs looking for? Here are some questions they will be asking.

Can the founder or CEO sell? He or she needs to be able to sell equity in the company to top investors, sell the product to customers (a no-brainer) and sell to potential employees. Can they attract talent away from secure, well-paid jobs at bigger companies?

Will the founders listen and take advice? Can we work with them, and do they understand that there are areas where they are weak and will need help?

How resilient are they? Can they cope with the stress of going from a small start-up to something much bigger? Will they burn out? How will they respond to stress?

Does their business plan fit our model? A VC fund is responsible to its own investors and needs to invest where there is a prospect of a good enough return to satisfy those investors.

All of these are areas where you can help your founders prepare themselves and become VC-ready.

Whenever new money comes in, the existing investors and founders need to do due diligence on the newcomers, whether angels or VCs, to make sure they are aligned with the vision and direction of the company. Ideally, the situation will be competitive, with several potential investors interested, and shareholders will be able to pick and choose the best fit.

> 'Some people are very reluctant to work with VCs, but I find them relatively easy to work with. You know they are behaving logically, in most cases trying to optimise return. You might disagree with their decisions, but their mentality is very consistent.'
>
> Andy Phillipps, entrepreneur and investor

I agree with Andy that VCs are essentially logical and consistent – after all investing is their business – but they're still people (whatever some might say) and there's always an element of unpredictability when people make decisions. Angels can act like consumers at times; they can be just as fickle as a consumer faced with an array of choices. But don't assume that VCs are robots guided only by algorithms.

> Things are moving on. You've found some entrepreneurs, met some other potential investors, and begun to drill down into the business plan and whether or not you think the founders can make it work. You're getting dangerously close to taking the plunge and investing, so it's time to talk about the legal formalities, the paperwork you need to get things up and running.

INVESTED INVESTOR TAKEAWAY

- Don't invest on your own – find co-investors to share the financial and administrative load.
- Do due diligence on the entrepreneurs and the business plan, and also on your co-investors.
- Start small – three to four co-investors is right at the very beginning.
- Don't be the deal lead until you are ready and confident that you know what to do.
- Make sure that the deal lead is the person most suited to the opportunity.
- Reach a mutually agreed valuation that is as justifiable as possible under the circumstances.

AN ENTREPRENEUR'S STORY:
When co-investing goes wrong and you have to fire your co-founder on his first day in the office

Gonçalo de Vasconcelos had already worked as an engineer and set up his own business by the time he came to Cambridge to take an MBA at Cambridge Judge Business School. While working in London with business angels and VCs, he had seen many exciting companies struggling to put together a funding round, and many people looking to invest in exactly those types of businesses. In the early days of crowdfunding, somehow these businesses and investors weren't connecting.

Gonçalo started to develop the concept for Syndicate Room. It wasn't simply to be another crowdfunding platform where investors and entrepreneurs could meet online; the model for Syndicate Room was that any funding rounds would be investor-led. Gonçalo had a strong sense that many investors new to the concept wanted to invest alongside business angels and other experienced investors. Nothing would be opened to investment unless it had been pre-qualified by an experienced investor, whether angel, VC or other professional investor, and that person or group would commit to investing in the business.

The first round of funding, around £15,000, was stretched out over a few months as Gonçalo worked on the technology and the legal framework for this new type of platform. A second family and friends round got the project ready to launch in 2013 and Gonçalo started work on the third round. By now, it was time to bring someone else on board, and Tom Britton agreed to join Gonçalo. Their agreement was that Tom would be co-founder, and Gonçalo got on with raising the third round ready for Tom to join.

On Tom's first day in the office, the third funding round, of £180,000, was seemingly in the bag, with most of the funds in an escrow account. Gonçalo was shocked to get a phone call from one of the investors who said they were changing the terms of the deal. The other co-investors were taken by surprise and the whole deal fell through. Gonçalo had to break the news to Tom, fire him, and then ask him to work for free. Syndicate Room had 48 hours before the money ran out; the £180,000 that was going to enable them finally to start building the business was gone, and Gonçalo was never going to work with that particular investor again.

'We had two days to rebuild a funding round that had taken over six months to build in the first place.'

The rest of the existing investors were supportive and offered funds but couldn't get to the amount needed to close the round. It was August, the height of the holiday season, and somehow Gonçalo had to find the rest of the money. He called Cambridge Angel Jonathan Milner. Milner already knew Gonçalo and Syndicate Room but hadn't been interested in investing because it didn't fit his investment criteria – it was too early stage and not in his sector. But this time, he agreed to invest – with the proviso that he wouldn't be involved or join the Board, as he was too busy running his own, highly successful company, Abcam.

Syndicate Room was saved and the rest, as they say, is history. Gonçalo and Tom began to build the team slowly, the platform started to gain traction in 2014, and has since gone on to win numerous awards. By early 2018, over 100 companies had raised nearly £120 million through Syndicate Room.

CHAPTER 6

The paperwork

All your efforts to meet entrepreneurs and find some like-minded angels to invest with have so far been aimed at reaching this point – doing the paperwork to make the arrangement formal and binding. This is when you will hand over the money and launch your entrepreneurs into the next exciting phase of growing their business. Not surprisingly, there is plenty to think about in drawing up and finalising the documents that will form the backbone of your continuing relationship with the new company. I'm afraid there's no way to make this chapter exciting, so feel free to skip to Chapter 7 and come back here later if you're not ready to delve into the nitty-gritty of paperwork.

The essentials
There are three essential legal documents in an investor/investee relationship:
- Shareholders' agreement, also known as the investment agreement (IA) or subscription agreement (SA)
- Articles of association
- Disclosure letter

In addition to these, you will need service agreements and possibly key man insurance.

But the key to getting these three documents right is the term sheet.

The term sheet
The term sheet is a mostly non-binding statement of intent that defines the deal the parties will complete. You, your fellow investors and the entrepreneurs will work together to produce a term sheet that all parties can accept.

Once you have a term sheet that everyone has agreed with and signed, it is unlikely to fail. The trick is in getting to a term sheet that is acceptable to all. An early term sheet drafted after preliminary due diligence, even if the valuation is provisional, can quickly reveal whether a deal is viable or not. Early warning that a deal is not likely to work can save everyone spending more time on detailed due diligence.

The term sheet includes elements that the investors will want to control as the company gets off the ground, especially if the entrepreneurs have little or no experience. However, some entrepreneurs have a lot of difficulty with this and feel they're becoming puppets rather than partners. If your entrepreneurs do not understand that they will inevitably lose some aspects of control once they take your investment, then they are probably not ready to take outside funding. Or you may have to educate them as part of the initial due diligence process, before you get to the term sheet stage.

The term sheet will be unique to the investment, so no two term sheets are the same. You can find plenty of sample term sheets on the internet, but be careful to check context and jurisdiction if you want to use any of them. I have developed a term sheet template over the decade or so since I started angel investing, but it is still evolving and I often have to tweak it in some way.

My term sheet template

- Investment
- Conditions of investment
- Terms of investment
- Confidentiality
- Applicable law
- Expiry date
- Exclusivity
- No intention to create legal relations
- Exclusion of representations and warranties
- Signature pages
- Appendices

I'm going to unpick these below, but always remember that this is an evolving and changeable list – another reason why you should invest alongside experienced angels when you start out.

Investment This section will specify the round (first, second, etc.), the amount, the type of shares the investors will receive in exchange for their money, and the percentage of the company they will own. In the UK, it should also cover whether or not the investment qualifies for EIS or SEIS tax relief and any obligations on the part of the founders to comply with HMRC regulations regarding EIS and SEIS.

The investment section is where you describe shareholdings and directorships, that is, who owns what percentage of the company already, and whether there are any senior appointments to be made (for example, an independent chair) that will include new shareholdings.

Pre-money and post-money valuations should be covered, price per share for investors, and whether there is an option pool and its size.

Practical details should also be included, such as when the money will be handed over to the founders (possibly through a lawyer's client account); how the money will be used by the company (for instance, whether or not it can be used to pay off any directors' loans); and an estimated completion date for the deal.

Conditions of investment This section will include items that the investment might be conditional on, such as completion of a shareholders' agreement, anti-money-laundering checks, completion of due diligence to everyone's satisfaction, service agreements for employees, (S)EIS clearance, IP consents, etc.

Terms of investment The investment terms section is important because it sets out how things will work between the company and the investors after the investment is completed.

It might include a number of warranties and disclosures, which are often found listed as an appendix. The warranties list includes things like proof of intellectual property (IP) ownership, insurance, contracts with external parties, etc.

Terms of investment also cover the composition of the Board and the appointment of a Board observer, who will play a key role as an intermediary between the company and the investors. Timing and frequency of Board meetings, and who is entitled to vote and how (for example, by proxy) when there are important decisions to be made, should also be included. The types of decisions that require such a vote may be listed as another appendix.

An important aspect is information – how will you know what is going on? Term sheets may well contain details about how, and how often, you and your fellow investors should be kept up to date with financial and operational information.

The founders should also feature in the terms of the investment – what their obligations are (for instance, specifying that they can't take consultancy work on the side), non-competition and confidentiality agreements, and confirming that the IP belongs to the company. There may be provisions concerning any shares owned by the founders, again often listed as an appendix.

Who pays for legal fees and other expenses necessary to complete the investment round, sometimes with caps on fees, should also be agreed so that there aren't any nasty surprises later on.

Confidentiality It should be obvious that the term sheet is confidential, but this should be stated in black and white as protection. It is also often helpful to have separate non-disclosure and non-circumvention agreements in place in parallel with the term sheet as added security, and to allow the more detailed and sensitive aspects of due diligence to proceed.

Applicable law You need to know which national laws and jurisdictions will govern the term sheet and later agreements, such as England and Wales, or Scotland.

Expiry date Fourteen days is a reasonable length of time to allow both parties to confirm that they accept the term sheet.

Exclusivity Naturally, investors who sign the term sheet will expect that things will proceed in an orderly manner and there won't be any surprises in the form of new investors coming in at a later date or the founders suddenly deciding to sell the company before the term sheet is signed (an extreme example but one I have experienced). Typically, exclusivity will be for a period of six to eight weeks.

No intention to create legal relations While some elements of the term sheet, such as confidentiality and applicable law, are legally binding, much of it is not and it cannot be taken as the legal contract for the investment.

Exclusion of representations and warranties This aims to ensure that no other agreements are in place that might affect the investment.

Signature pages The CEO, or an agreed person who can sign on behalf of the company, and the deal lead sign the term sheet. Sometimes, all pledged investors need to sign, but this is cumbersome and rare.

Appendices Some of the elements in the term sheet give rise to lists that are better separated and defined in appendices. These include:
- Rights attaching to ordinary shares
  These may include voting, dividends, liquidation, sale of assets, sale of shares, pre-emption rights on new issues and transfers, co-sales and drag-alongs.
- Warranties
  Warranties are there to ensure that the founders have provided accurate information on all aspects of the company that the investors need in order to make an informed investment decision. Warranties may cover, among other things: share capital, group structure, information, agreements, commitments and liabilities, IP, employment and consultancy arrangements, contracts with external parties, assets and debts, litigation, taxation, statutory and legal requirements and insurance.
- Important decisions
  It should be specified where a decision requires agreement from a defined majority of investors or investor director consent – although you should also be careful to add a proviso for other

items that you might not list here but that might come up. The list of potentially important decisions might include altering rights, changing the share capital, altering the articles of association, declaring dividends, buying or selling shares in another company, winding up the company, agreeing budgets and forecasts, capital expenditure above a certain level, selling any assets above a certain level, changing the business model, setting up new offices or branches, appointing an employee or consultant at a total cost above a threshold level, or entering into significant contracts that could have a major effect on the business if they run into difficulty.

- Rights attaching to shares held by the founders
  These include vesting rights, the definition of a bad leaver and what happens to the shares they own, including valuations. We'll look at bad leavers in more detail later.

The shareholders' agreement

The shareholders' agreement is the legally binding document that reflects what has been agreed in the term sheet and provides the detail on who owns how much of the company (and when). It is drafted by lawyers and based on the term sheet. Lawyers are expensive and you want your money to be directed towards growing the company, so the more solid the term sheet is, the easier – and quicker – it is for the shareholders' agreement to be drawn up.

When your investment goes into a start-up, you receive a share of ownership in the company to reflect your investment. The founders will have a much larger share but you pay for yours with money, they pay for theirs with so-called sweat equity, that is, their hard work, vision and drive. One way of looking at this is that the investors are buying shares in the founding team, where the value of the team is the pre-money valuation. Essentially, if no more investment rounds are needed, over a certain period of time the founders will have put in enough sweat equity to cover the value of their shares in the company. Investors might also introduce a reverse vesting clause for the founders, so that the founders earn their shares back over time, and this can be repeated in subsequent rounds, or when VCs come into the picture.

An option is the opportunity to buy a share or number of shares at a defined price at a future date. Options are used as a form of partial salary replacement in the early days of a company when cash is tight, and also as incentives for employees to encourage them to remain with the company and reach targets. In later rounds, investors can also put incentives in place for the founders in terms of options – the opportunity to increase their share of the company when, say, certain milestones are reached. This necessarily reduces the investors' percentage holding in the company, as they have to give a proportion of their ownership up to fulfil the options, but can be a key to future success.

It may be three to four years from when the options are granted to their being fully vested, or available to be exercised, although they may well have vested in stages during that time. Normally, the first year after options are granted is the cliff – the employee is not entitled to exercise any of their options for the first year (this can be thought of as an extended probation period) but at the end of that time, they are granted the entire first year's worth of options. Subsequently, the options vest or accrue at a pre-agreed rate over time. The employee can decide when – and indeed whether – to buy their options when they become vested.

It is very rare for employees to exercise their options until the company exits and all the shareholders are bought out, although this sometimes happens when employees are deemed good leavers (discussed in more detail below).

If an employee exercises their options early, the company will still be very young and the risks are still high – most companies that fail do so in their first five years. Essentially, exercising options at this stage is equivalent to writing the company a cheque as a gift, rather than making a strategic investment decision. There will also be problems if the employee then decides to leave the company before it exits, as there will be no market for their shares. If the employee waits, they will also see whether their options actually end up underwater, that is, the options cost more than the sales value of the shares at exit. There's no point in buying shares for more than they are currently worth – and a weaker valuation says plenty about the status of the company. Generally at exit, all options must be exercised or they simply cease to exist.

To make matters more complicated, there are different classes of share. The investors' and founders' shares might be different from those offered as options to employees, and different again from those offered to non-executive directors or other members of the Board. While the size of the option pool will have been decided in the shareholders' agreement, any option agreements will be separate and governed by a number of factors, including number of rounds to date and whether or not preference shares have been granted.

In addition, there are different tax implications for the owners of options. For employees in the UK, something called the Enterprise Management Incentive, or EMI, is a scheme that makes options tax-efficient for qualifying employees, and currently covers share options to a value of up to £250,000 over a three-year period for companies with assets of £30 million or less. Some activities are excluded, such as banking and farming, and employees are defined by certain criteria – such as hours worked, existence of an employment contract – in order to qualify for the scheme. The UK government currently states that 'A person may be an employee in employment law but have a different status for tax purposes', so it's not straightforward.

Articles of association
Articles of association are essentially the rules defining how the company will be operated. They are typically based on standard

formats and UK company law. Articles of association are often mentioned together with the memorandum of association, which is the document that commits the signatories – the founders – to form the company. Once the company has been registered, the memorandum of association cannot be altered.

Model articles for UK companies can be found on the government website, www.gov.uk, along with a range of other information on the paperwork and processes involved in setting up a company.

Articles of association are frequently altered to align with the term sheet. For that reason, I don't look at the articles of association during due diligence, because they will almost certainly change. When everything is ready to sign, I check that the shareholders' agreement and articles of association are consistent with the term sheet.

The disclosure letter

The disclosure letter is extremely important because this is where the founders demonstrate that they meet the warranties included in the term sheet (and therefore shareholders' agreement). The letter will include general and specific disclosures, supported by the relevant documents as evidence (sometimes referred to as the disclosure bundle).

Disclosure letters include a list of all the things the shareholders might want to see, so that the entrepreneurs are unlikely to be challenged later for not revealing something – another instance where transparency is crucial. Disclosure letters are useful because they make the entrepreneurs think through the different aspects of the business very carefully, and also make them aware of the penalties if they get it wrong.

In the first round of an early stage start-up, there shouldn't be much to disclose, but the disclosure letter will be more relevant in the second and subsequent rounds.

I have only heard of one occasion where a warranty was challenged. After considerable legal costs and board conflict, the founder responded by shutting the company down, losing money for everyone.

Service agreements and key man insurance

Service agreements might cover the conditions of employment for the founder directors. Start-ups are often launched with no contracts of employment or job descriptions, the two or three co-founders simply doing everything that is needed between them. But at the point at which the company receives investment, more formal arrangements are needed to ensure that everyone knows what is expected of them and that the position should they leave is clear. Such agreements can also help to ensure that the founders are aligned with the investors.

Shareholdings, good leaver/bad leaver provisions and other potential hazards can be part of a service agreement. In my sector, they might also include references to ownership of intellectual property, such as patents, trademarks and copyrights.

Key man insurance is always important for me as the company is dependent on the founders. Remember that story of the guy in the wingsuit? It can be expensive to insure against dangerous sports, but if the company is dependent, at least in the early stages, on two or three people and their ideas, it might be essential.

The question of lawyers

I've mentioned that I believe a young company needs to put all its resources into getting up and running, so personally I like to see the cost of lawyers minimised as much as possible. Nevertheless, things must be done properly.

Invested investors generally expect to represent themselves in early rounds. This is one of the places where their prior experience is essential, and why new angels should align themselves with more experienced co-investors. I always require that the entrepreneurs are represented by a lawyer, who will not only draft and agree the legals, but also educate the entrepreneurs on what they mean.

In later rounds, which will almost certainly involve much larger sums of money and probably additional investors, it will be time to call in the lawyers for all parties.

Invested investors will have worked with legal teams in the past and will have developed relationships with lawyers they know and trust. They will make the introductions when it is time for lawyers to get involved, and will reasonably expect the legal advisors to be fair, even though they will be representing the company rather than the investors.

The term sheet will – should – have specified that the company itself will bear the costs of investor legal advice when it becomes necessary, so that the investors are not suddenly presented with extra expenses on top of their investment in the company.

I always recommend that it's best not to have lawyers on both sides in the early stages if this can be avoided. They may spend too much time (which equals money) talking to each other.

Good leaver/bad leaver

Good leaver/bad leaver is shorthand for the various classifications of founders and employees at the point at which they leave a start-up. People leave for all sorts of reasons, but for a start-up, the departure of one of the founders can create all sorts of complications even if you have made provisions from the beginning.

It's a very important concept to think about and get right in the term sheet, the founding documents of the company and the shareholder agreements. There are several issues involved, and you will have to think both forwards and backwards at the same time to cover all eventualities, or at least as many as possible.

The situation when a founder leaves a start-up is complicated by a number of factors. These include what percentage of the company they own already, if they hold any options to buy more shares in the company at a future date, and the valuation of the company not only when their options were defined, but also on the date they leave the company. All that has to be prepared for as far in advance as possible, against the eventuality that a founder might leave early, before the company has really got going, or before its chances of survival are fully understood.

Why do you have to think about what might happen down the line, when one of the founders leaves? Perhaps this story will show you why.

Paul Allen, described by *Wired* magazine as the 'accidental zillionaire', co-founded Microsoft with Bill Gates in 1975. Despite dual founders traditionally owning their company 50/50, Gates and Allen ultimately negotiated an ownership arrangement that gave Gates 64% of the company and Allen the remaining 36%, something Allen claimed was more to do with his lack of negotiating skills than reflecting actual input in the early days. Whatever the reason for the share split, Allen still owned a sizeable proportion of the company.

This led to trouble when Allen left in 1983. He had been diagnosed with Hodgkin's lymphoma in 1982 and had undergone successful treatment, but decided he no longer wanted to be part of the stressful environment at a rapidly growing Microsoft. With no provision for this situation in place, Gates offered to buy Allen's shares, but Allen was not obliged to sell. He refused Gates' low offer for the shares, and retained not only his 36% ownership, but also his seat on the Board. Allen became a billionaire when Microsoft listed on NASDAQ in 1986, and is now worth over $20 billion.

One can imagine all sorts of scenarios that might play out in a start-up that ends up one-third owned by someone no longer involved in the day-to-day life of the company. At the very least the remaining founders could well feel that their hard work was ultimately rewarding someone else who is neither contributing to the growth of the company nor suffering from all the hardships and stress that involves. Had Gates been able to buy back Allen's shares, he might have used them to attract senior employees and more skills, making the journey easier – mind you, Microsoft hasn't done too badly even without Allen's help, but that level of success is rare in itself.

Hence the idea of founders as good leavers and bad leavers. What kind of leaver was Allen? Let's look at how the different types of founder leavers are defined and the implications for future ownership and running of the company.

Founders leave positions for a variety of reasons. Some have to depart through no fault of their own, for instance if they become ill, like Paul Allen, or even die. They might have to resign because a spouse has to move to another country for work, or one of their children becomes sick, or simply because they have given up on their original vision for the company and think they'd be better off elsewhere. Finally, a founder might be asked to leave because of poor performance or, in the worst-case scenario, gross misconduct.

Good leavers are those who leave through redundancy (very unlikely for a founder, but possible for an employee) or illness, or sometimes through resignation (if they are considered to have given sufficient years' service to the company to be classed as good leavers). Bad leavers are those who leave intentionally without a mitigating reason or without having served the company long enough, or who have to be fired. These distinctions have to be set out in the documentation from the beginning, so that if any such situations arise, there are clear-cut ways to deal with them.

A bad leaver might be defined as 'a founder who ceases to be an employee, director or consultant of the Company within a period of three years of completion of the Investment by reason of: (a) voluntarily resigning or (b) dismissal by the Company by reason of breach of contract or (c) if he or she is neither an employee nor a consultant but is in material breach of the schedule of actions... he or she has agreed to undertake... '.

The problem with all types of founder leavers is that they may well own, or have an option on, a share of the business. If they are no longer with the business, but retain a share of ownership, there are a number of implications. If they leave but keep their shares, and the business has a very advantageous exit, they end up profiting from everyone else's hard work. If they leave and keep their shares, even if it amounts to only a small percentage of the company, they may be in a position to block decisions that require unanimous or majority shareholder votes, even to the extent that they might block an exit. Being held to ransom like that could be a disaster, and is the reason for including drag-along clauses (where the majority shareholders can force minority shareholders to sell their shares at exit) in the documentation.

As noted in the Paul Allen example, if the departing founder keeps shares, then those left behind end up working for their erstwhile colleague as well as for themselves. If the departure was due to a major falling out between founders, this can leave a very bad taste.

A resigning good founder leaver might be permitted to keep shares, particularly if they have made a major contribution to the company, and if their share does not amount to a large percentage ownership of the company. This will be a Board decision – provision for which should be included in the documentation. Generally, good leavers do keep all their shares but, if the cash is available, may sell some back to the company at a fair value, which reflects the current valuation and their contributions.

A bad founder leaver must give up all their shares and options on departure, returning any shares either at the price they paid for them, or at current agreed face value.

Now we come to the tricky question of valuation – how much does each share or share option cost? Deciding how much each share is worth for a private company is difficult when there is no market for the shares and the leaver is seeking the maximum they can extract at a time between investment rounds. But the valuation of an option has to be defensible because the EMI tax relief scheme requires the approval of HMRC. The company has to provide HMRC with supporting documents to justify the price they want to set for options, based on the valuation, and HMRC has to confirm that this price is acceptable.

All this serves to underscore how important it is to cover as many variations and definitions as possible in the documentation so that the company and its investors have a robust framework for dealing with complicated situations.

> There's one more thing you need to do before everything is in place, and that is develop the Board – or create one if it doesn't already exist. Even the smallest start-up needs a Board if it is to grow up one day to be a flourishing company. But who should be on the Board, and what will they be doing? Read on to find out.

INVESTED INVESTOR TAKEAWAY
- The three essential legal documents are the shareholders' agreement, the articles of association and the disclosure letter.
- Service agreements and key man insurance may be important.
- The term sheet is the crucial foundation document for the shareholders' agreement and articles of association.
- Don't forget to include good leaver/bad leaver provisions.

AN INVESTOR'S STORY:
Has there ever been an interesting story about paperwork?

I'd prefer to end this chapter like all the others, with a story from an entrepreneur or an investor about their adventures along this part of the journey. Unfortunately, the paperwork, the legal documents, should never be the source of amusing anecdotes, otherwise you're in trouble. The legals are there for a reason, not for when things are going well but for when they are going wrong. So instead, here are a couple of examples that reinforce how important it is to get the paperwork right in the first place – and at the exit. First of all, a salutary lesson on the importance of the legal foundations of the arrangement when the founders fall out.

However wise and invested an investor you are, you can't predict the path of human relationships, and co-founders who are full of vim and vigour in the early days may find the stresses and strains of running a start-up hard to deal with. It's difficult to prevent a situation where the founders fall out, but always a risk in this high-pressure world.

In one instance, one of two co-founders ended up hating the other so much that they tried to bring the entire company down. The disgruntled co-founder sent information – trade secrets – to a third party (outside the company) and was suspended for gross misconduct. Then they threatened a libel suit for defamation. To make matters worse, they owned a significant share of the company and the Board could not suspend their voting rights, even though they were suspended from the company.

The lesson? Use lawyers who know what they're doing and understand the challenges of early stage investing so that this situation – or at least the fallout – is manageable if it ever arises.

In a similar example, a founder who was setting up his first business and had never seen a shareholder agreement before, relied mostly on common sense and the internet, with a bit of legal help. Later, he realised that wasn't good enough – there were mistakes and they were costly to correct. Next time, he'll invest in a good lawyer from the outset.

On the other hand, some paperwork that seems onerous or unwelcome at the exit can be a blessing in disguise. Exit conditions when a company is acquired frequently include locking the founders and key team members in so they don't leave for at least a couple of years, and/or preventing them from selling some or all of the shares they may receive as part of the exit deal. In Chapter 10 you'll find the story of Active Hotels, an example where being obliged to invest in the acquiring business was a bonus, as the share price went up and the exit deal continued to improve long after the paperwork was signed.

CHAPTER 7

Putting the Board together

I've talked about transparency and building trust. A strong relationship between investors and founders could be the difference between success and failure, but however much you trust and value each other's contributions, there must still be a formal mechanism for overseeing developments. It's time to talk about the Board.

How hands-on should you be?

It shouldn't be assumed that an optimum model for running the company will emerge automatically from the fact that investors and entrepreneurs share the same goals.

Many entrepreneurs have never run a company before, so they want guidance from investors who bring experience and skills as well as money – often referred to as having 'grey hair'. I think that's a rather misleading term as you don't have to be old or grey-haired to have had experiences and developed skills that make you useful to a start-up company, so I prefer BTDT (been there, done that) or 'seasoned', as some interactions can be quite peppery.

> 'I think angels might be surprised at how open companies are to having advice. Particularly in a university environment, because you've got two types of founders. You've got career academics who don't want to be the CEO of a company and so are looking for someone to work with them and take the lead and give advice, whether that's at board level or CEO level or whatever. And you've got the young team of graduates or students who are keen and eager to learn but don't have enough grey hairs or experience, and they are super keen to get people involved as mentors and as angels to guide their journey. They're just great to work with, because they have so much enthusiasm and the best of those will really listen and take on board what you're telling them.'
>
> Anne Dobrée, Head of Seed Funds,
> Cambridge Enterprise

Before the investment deal closes and the money is transferred, the extent to which investors and others, such as advisors, will be involved in the company should be agreed and noted in the legal documents. This ranges from the very fundamental composition of the Board to frequency of contacts and updates to investors. But be aware – crowdfunding is different and your involvement with companies you fund via this method will not be the same, and in some cases will be unsatisfactory

Many investors in the US and some early stage VCs do not believe in a Board and let the entrepreneurial team run the company until an A round of funding. That may work for founders who are on their second or third start-up, with a success behind them, but I feel strongly that the monitoring, governance and mentoring that a Board brings is essential.

The extent of involvement starts with what is set out in the term sheet. The invested investor, sophisticated angels and VCs will always want – and indeed should demand – to be involved, not only to keep an eye on how their money is being used, but also because they should have strong sector-specific knowledge or experience to share that can help the company grow. The rhythm of a formal reporting structure also helps the founders and their senior leadership team to focus on what needs to be done and when, and provides valuable collateral for future funding rounds and eventual exit.

Above all, it is imperative to create a Board that has the right balance of founders, investors and independents to ensure that everyone contributes appropriately and in a timely manner.

 'If you don't believe the chief executive can make a good decision, then you shouldn't be on the Board.'

Andy Phillipps, entrepreneur and investor

Board composition

So who do you want on your Board? You want people who will add value. Naturally, you want representation from both the investors and the founders, with each side nominating an agreed number of directors. Investors may also be able to nominate one or more Board observers, who won't have voting rights but will act as a channel for information flow between the Board and the investor group as a whole, plus should have other skills useful to the company. The

Board might want to appoint an independent director as well, who might be the logical choice for Board chair.

> Syndicate Room has a particularly good Board, including a serial entrepreneur, a lawyer and a banker, so pretty much all the bases are covered.

The term sheet should specify how many directors there will be on the Board, and how those directors will be chosen. It might specify a maximum number of directors, which allows leeway to have fewer if appropriate, and where those directors should be drawn from.

Both investors and founders should be able to nominate a certain number of directors. Investors who put in more – owning say 10% or more of the shares – may have a greater say over director appointments, while those who put in less (commonly owning 5%–10%) might be able to nominate a Board observer.

But Boards also need to be agile and this is best achieved if they are not too large. Hence investors may not always appoint as many directors as they are theoretically entitled to, given their shareholdings in the company. In my view, in the very early days, with a founding team of two, a Board of three is fine, with senior management (as they are recruited) joining part of the Board meetings. The Board will grow with VC funding, as their investment will come with representation and stipulations regarding Board membership.

So who's who on the Board?
Directors Those in charge, including some or all of the founders and representatives from among the investors. In the UK, all directors will be registered with Companies House as Board members, giving them legal responsibilities, and putting their names in the public domain. All directors are obliged to attend all Board

meetings. Remember, the founders are employees – the company is managed by the Board and not vice versa.

Founder director(s) Those chosen from among and by the founders of the company, commonly all the founders at the start.

Investor directors One or more of the investors (but usually only one), chosen by the group of investors to represent their interests on the Board. They will have the ability to veto some actions.

Board observers Representatives of the investors who provide input to the Board but don't have voting rights, and who report back to the investors. They should receive most of the Board communications, such as the Board information pack, including trading updates and status reports. Observers are not obliged to attend every Board meeting, but are not passive, as the name suggests. Observers are expected to be fully engaged and contribute when they do attend.

Chair of the Board Often an independent director, chosen by mutual agreement by the founder director(s) and the investor director(s). There are arguments for and against the chair being a shareholder. The argument for is that the chair is fully aligned with the shareholder value growth of the company; against is the lack of true independence that being a shareholder brings.

The shareholder agreement should specify how many Board meetings are required each year. If the entrepreneurs delay one or more Board meetings, it could be a signal that something is wrong.

There should also be a date to review the composition of the Board. It takes a while for a start-up to get going, and it is useful to review the Board after a year to make sure it is providing the necessary direction and support. It may be that additional expertise needs to be brought on to the Board, or that the Board is actually too large to fulfil its role effectively. There are legal responsibilities, too, such as protecting creditors, so it is important to have these provisions in place.

In the short term (perhaps until the second funding round), Board meetings might be held every month, then every six or eight weeks. From my experience, Board meetings with younger first-time entrepreneurs can take up to four or five hours, with two hours being taken up with normal business and the rest being mentoring and coaching.

Producing a Board pack and attending a two- or three-hour Board meeting can seem quite a lot of work for the entrepreneurs, since it adds up to at least half a day per founder. But it has corporate and personal benefits. For instance, producing a structured Board pack helps the founders maintain an overview of the company and how it is doing. It can also guide them in reflecting on where things are going well and where they might need support or coaching to improve their own or others' performance.

The Board pack will include minutes of the previous meeting. There is no standard format for minutes, so they can vary from a set of actions (possibly using an online collaborative tool such as Asana, Slack, etc.) to a multi-page document with discussions. Of course, length and style of minutes also depends on the audience. I very much like to see a full set of previous Board minutes in the due diligence pack for a future round (which is not easily achieved if using an online tool). At the other extreme, verbose minutes can lead to time-consuming questions from potential new investors.

Sample Board agenda

1. Conflicts of interest (seems formal but may become more important later as the Board grows). For instance, some of my portfolio companies are customers of one of the companies I chair.

2. Accepting minutes of last meeting
3. Actions arising (unless covered elsewhere in the agenda)
4. Sales report* – brief overview of items that the Board needs to hear: lost orders or sales (and the reasons), contacts needed, partners/re-sellers, sales pipeline, foreign forays, successes
5. Marketing report*
6. Technology report*
7. Human resources (HR) report*
8. Finance report*§
9. Infrastructure* – premises, IT, insurance, health and safety compliance, etc.
10. Risk register* – informal early on, becoming more formal later
11. Strategy – probably to discuss output from the advisory panel, if there is one, although the Board needs to own and adopt the outcomes formally
12. Any other business
13. Date/time/place of next meeting

* Reports and information pertinent to these items should be sent out to Board members several days ahead of the meeting. Too often the pack arrives late the night before. This is bad practice, but founders have many priorities, and I too commonly read the board pack on the train journey to the meeting.

§ The finance report should include profit and loss (year to date and last month, both against budget), balance sheet to end of previous month, creditors, debtors and cash flow forecast (quarterly). I am very keen on seeing how debtors (assuming trade credit is given) are ageing (i.e. which customers are more than a month overdue in paying), as this may show the company is invoicing too early, that customers are not happy with what the company is providing, or that the company is not chasing customers for money (too many businesses wait until they are chased for payment, even the multinational ones). Remember that customer money is much better in your bank account than theirs and no investor wants to provide equity to cover working capital – that should be provided by customers.

A note about voting. Since Board observers don't have a vote, you might wonder if they serve a useful function for the company.

Normal Board behaviour is to make decisions based on one vote per director. A lot of things are discussed at Board meetings, but decisions at this level should be big picture issues and not day-to-day management stuff, so voting might be needed – but not always. Some issues can be minuted as 'no vote needed', while others can be classed as an 'implied unanimous vote', that is, everyone agrees and so no vote is actually taken. It is good practice to confirm unanimity in the minutes, since this serves to flush out any disagreements so that unanimity can be minuted, and will help to avoid issues in the future. The Board observer will have been part of the discussions and their views and advice will have been heard.

The ideal situation is consensus, where the founders and investors are aligned, and votes aren't needed.

The functions of the Board

Let's take a closer look at what the Board is expected to do. I mentioned monitoring, governance and mentoring.

Monitoring involves making sure that information is flowing freely between the company and the investors, and is a key role for the investor director.

❝ I'm an evangelist for honest and transparent information flow between investors and entrepreneurs. Without it, I think it's extremely rare (if not impossible) for a company to be successful to the point where all parties involved are happy. This is one of the reasons why I insist that all my portfolio companies have an investor director on the Board.

If the investors don't know what is going on, they may well wonder if the founders are doing what they said they would be doing in their business plan. They may worry that their investment is at risk – or rather, at even greater risk than it is anyway – or feel that they're not being asked for help when their input could be most beneficial.

Silence can be ominous. Are the founders not communicating with the investors because things are going so well that they are incredibly busy and don't have time? Or are they keeping quiet because things are going wrong and they don't want to admit it? Whichever it is, there's never any excuse for not communicating; even if the company is in a busy but very positive stage, it shouldn't be that difficult to send a quick email to say, 'Things going fantastically, full update next month' or similar. Where things are not going so well, it's far better to ask investors for help and advice than continue to struggle in silence – after all, invested investors want to help and be part of a successful venture that brings benefits to the world.

I get very concerned if I don't hear from my companies on a regular basis, and I expect quarterly updates as well as any ad hoc communications. The shareholders' update might not be enough, especially when things are moving fast and the founders need extra help. The team don't have to send me a report longer than three or four pages, but I need to be kept up to date on the key markers – the key performance indicators, or KPIs.

What do you need in an update? I'm tempted to say, 'If you don't know what should be in a financial update to shareholders, you shouldn't be investing in or starting a company'. But we all begin somewhere, and you should never be afraid to ask. The shareholders' update is effectively a heavily cut down version of board packs.

The box that follows includes the basics that I would expect to see in an update.

> ## What I expect in a shareholders' update
> ### Portfolio Co Ltd: Report to Investors March 20XX
>
> 1. Executive summary
>   What is our 'ask'? How can the shareholders help? There doesn't have to be an ask, but most shareholders love being able to help and it makes them feel they are on the same journey.
>   What are the highlights of the year to date? Reaching profitability? Milestones? R&D grants or other awards? Key personnel hires?
>   What are the overall financials? How much cash is there in the bank? What is the cash runway? What are the latest revenue figures? Are there profits on sales? What is the target for the year? When is the next equity round needed? Remember that, until a company reaches breakeven, the losses need to be funded by equity (potentially plus grants). How is product development progressing?
>   What is the bigger picture? Regulatory environment, approvals, wider economic situation?
> 2. Sales strategy and distribution
>   How is the sales strategy reflecting the business model? Has either had to be adapted due to changing circumstances? Who is/are the key figure(s) driving sales? What shareholder input might be useful?
>   How is/are distribution channels developing? Is progress slow, fast, as expected? Are there any roadblocks in the distribution channels?
>   Is there progress in international distribution? If so, what has happened since the last update?

3. Marketing, PR and direct sales approaches
   What marketing activities have been undertaken? What feedback/response has been recorded? What metrics are being used to track effectiveness?
   How is PR integrated with marketing? What media coverage has been secured? Are there any new relationships developing with key journalists, media outlets or spokespeople?
   What are the website, social media and other online metrics? Where are leads coming from?
4. Product development and procurement
   How is product development going? How are industry standards being met? How are innovations outside industry standards being met by the industry and customers?
   If appropriate, has there been progress in manufacturing? Where is manufacturing taking place? How are manufacturing costs in comparison to previous expectations? What are the logistics around product delivery? What areas have been noted for improvement? There may also be quality and customer service metrics to evaluate.
5. Financials – against forecasts and budget, and may include financial KPI tracking.
   Cash in the bank
   Sales figures
   Gross margin
   P&L
   Balance sheet against budget
   Forecast for the next quarter
   Projections for revenues and how those revenues, if realised, might be used to grow the company

> And most importantly, if not at breakeven, what is the runway – the time until the cash runs out and either more money has been raised or the company closes.
> 6. Can you help?
> An extended version of the 'ask' in the executive summary. What might the investors do to help the company? What introductions could they make that would be useful at this stage? Can they help source needed skills?

There may not be much to report from one update to the next but the financials will always have moved, and there's almost bound to be at least one other thing to report – new hires, a new marketing activity that has gone live, or a key sale that has been secured or fallen through. If the latter, letting the investors know quickly gives them the opportunity to help, especially if it was a sales lead that originally came from one of them.

Keeping investors updated is an overhead, and it isn't a trivial exercise, but the benefits far outweigh the effort put in. Updates force the entrepreneurs to reflect on what they are doing and their progress. They also help them to keep on top of all the different factors that indicate whether things are going in the right direction. Providing advice based on the update helps to show the entrepreneurs that you are keen to be an asset and not a liability.

> In my portfolio, I have investees that report every month, every quarter, every year and never. If never, then the chance of my re-investing in that business is zero.

Governance is all about ensuring that the company is compliant with existing regulations around not only the products and any certifications they require, but also around employment law, tax regimes, data protection, health and safety and all the rest of the red tape involved in running a company. One important task within the first two years will be to set up a remuneration committee, which will oversee remuneration for the founders and the use of the option pool. This group is typically a sub-committee of the Board, but may include one or more of the directors, one shareholder who is not on the Board and/or another independent person who does not have a conflict of interest.

Mentoring is about how the investors help the entrepreneurs develop and reach their goals, to the mutual benefit of all concerned. The extent to which investors provide mentoring varies enormously, partly depending on the previous experience of the founders, and partly depending on what they are bringing to the party themselves.

Invested investors should be mentors, rarely coaches. In my view, the distinction between coaching and mentoring revolves around the interplay between each side. A coach has a collection of different coaching methods, a toolbox, if you like, and is trained to use all of them. But they will choose which tools to use depending on what they feel the coachee needs; the coach doesn't necessarily need to know anything about the business to choose the right tools. Once the coach has selected a tool, it serves as a metaphorical mirror, a means by which the coachee can reflect on their issue and move towards solving the problem for themselves. It can be a powerful way to help the coachee address an issue from a different, and enlightening, perspective.

Coaching can be helpful for specific personal development issues

Being an invested investor can take up a lot of your time, especially if you're like me and find it hard to say 'no' once you get involved in a project. Many angels are committed and passionate about what they do, and worry about the consequences if they turn down a request for help. They tend to have a similar dialogue going on inside their head – 'If I say no, I'm letting someone down/failing the business/failing my fellow investors'. But everyone's time is valuable, and should be used wisely, especially as a portfolio of investments grows.

A few years ago, I started working with a business coach to explore why I found it so hard to avoid overcommitting myself. I've come to learn that sometimes saying 'no' really means saying 'yes' to something else, where I can use my time more productively and add more value.

A mentor has an altogether different relationship with the entrepreneur – one of sharing and teaching based on their own experiences in similar situations. They might be able to pull out a specific example from a previous investment that will help the entrepreneur. The investor's experience will never be identical to what the entrepreneur is facing, but there will be key points that can be used to explore the issues so the entrepreneur will understand that they're not the only one who has ever gone through this experience, and that there are possible solutions. An invested investor acting as a mentor won't be prescriptive. They should never say, 'You must do this', but should talk through the situation and possible scenarios, best, worst or otherwise, that might ensue. The end goal is, to use a trendy phrase, empowerment. The aim is for the entrepreneur to come to their own decision about how to tackle the issue, helping them to grow and learn.

An angel who has recently exited from a CEO or other senior role must remember to be a mentor and not to push too hard – after all, the entrepreneurs are the ones running the business. But it's a delicate balance, because the business belongs to the shareholders, and both the angels and the entrepreneurs are the shareholders. Angels shouldn't keep quiet, but shouldn't dominate either.

What if there's a problem?

I like to think of a problem escalation ladder: founder(s)/chair/ investor director(s)/full Board/shareholders.

The founders should be the first to spot if things are going off course – if they don't spot a brewing problem, then that's a big warning signal to the investors. The founders should also be transparent and notify those who need to be notified – if they suspect something is amiss but don't admit to it, that's another warning signal. But I have a caveat on this aspect of transparency, which I'll explain below.

Ideally, the founders should try to solve the problem themselves, before it is escalated up the ladder. This is partly to do with time and efficiency – there's no point involving the Board if the problem can be nipped in the bud. I realise this goes partly against my credo of full transparency at all times, but sometimes it's appropriate to solve the problem first and then tell people about it afterwards if necessary. Not always, though. And sometimes, the entrepreneurs can be over-confident about their own problem-solving abilities where a little advice could help them make better decisions.

> **TRANSPARENCY TAKEAWAY**
>
> Sometimes it's appropriate to solve a problem first and then tell shareholders about it. This is one of the few instances where full transparency at all times could be a hindrance rather than a help.

One situation where it is critical to keep the Board up to date is cash. There are too many occasions when the entrepreneur fails to warn the shareholders that cash is getting low and then comes to them in a panic asking for more money. The shareholders may well refuse to put their hands back in their pockets when they get a last-minute request. If they had been forewarned, they might have been able to head off the problem, perhaps by helping to find a new customer or identifying where savings could be made, or more importantly being prepared to invest again, perhaps sooner than they had expected. It's very annoying when you can see a small issue that could easily have been resolved becoming a much more serious threat to the business.

What if you're not on the Board?

Not all investors can have a place on the Board – as I've said, the Board needs to be agile so should be kept to the smallest effective size and avoid duplicating skills and experience that are already represented.

But as a shareholder, the invested investor should naturally take an interest in how their investee company is doing. Not surprisingly, the extent of this varies tremendously. Some investors set up regular calls with the CEOs of all their investments, perhaps once a month, every quarter or just once a year. Others are happy to receive information on a more ad hoc basis, but I don't recommend this – if you have even a moderate-sized portfolio, it is easy for one or more of your companies to slip through the cracks if you sit back and wait for them to get in touch, rather than proactively checking on them.

Ad hoc contact in the other direction might also be important – the invested investor might have more time to scan the broader landscape and pick up useful information that the entrepreneurs might have missed. A quick email when something comes up is all that's needed. Similarly, the invested investor will always be on the look out for useful connections and introductions for their portfolio companies, and these should be followed through when they come up, rather than waiting for a scheduled call in a few months' time.

> 'A core part of the investing job is to maintain relationships. You never know how or when you might add value, so you need to keep talking to people. An important area where angels can add value is through serendipitous connections.'
>
> Rajat Malhotra, 2013 UK Angel Investor of the Year and managing partner, Wren Capital

Invested investors want to help build the business, so entrepreneurs must not take investor involvement as being nosy or interfering. But if communication channels aren't open, the investors might not know when their help is most needed, or when it is the right time to introduce a key contact. And potentially worse – imagine a scenario where I haven't been told that the sales director has left, and I try to introduce them to a potential customer. I look stupid, the company looks mismanaged and the introduction may fall flat.

But equally, invested investors don't want to pester their entrepreneurs unnecessarily. So rather than going straight to the entrepreneurs, my first point of call if I'm feeling out of the loop might be the investor director.

> **TRANSPARENCY TAKEAWAY**
> If I don't have sufficient information from my portfolio companies, I can't help them as much as I might.

Getting the balance right

In an ideal world, I get the right amount of information from my companies at the right time – the Goldilocks scenario, if you like. Sometimes, I get too much information – monthly updates from a company that we all know is going to grow slowly are probably too much, some of the information might not be useful, and too much information is also – too much. But it's more likely that I get too little information and have to chase them myself, and the reasons for this are two-fold.

First, I might not be getting any information because things are looking bad and the entrepreneur doesn't want or know how to tell me that, for instance, cash is running out. This is a big issue, because if the entrepreneurs come to the investors at the last minute, in a panic asking for more money, they are more than likely to be turned down, or be pushed into accepting money at a lower valuation – a down-round – because the investors will have lost trust in them. On the other hand, if the investors are kept well-informed, including about the cash situation, they might be better prepared to put more money into the company to help it get over a sticky patch.

The other reason I might be lacking information is because the entrepreneurs think they are too busy to provide a written update. Yes, being the founder of an early stage company is a 24/7 job, and taking the time to write a report for investors means stepping out of the race and changing to a different mode of thinking for a while, so many entrepreneurs view it as an inconvenience. But best practice in personal development always recommends taking time to reflect; collecting the evidence they need for an update to shareholders gives the entrepreneur time to reflect and truly understand how their company is doing. It is all too easy to rattle along in the rush of the day-to-day and never stop to look at the big picture.

Most importantly, the entrepreneur should train themselves always to put an 'ask' at the start and end of their update. 'We could do with an introduction to J P Morgan'; 'Do you know any supplier contacts in China?'; 'We're starting to look for a chief operating officer for the next stage, have you any suggestions?' Investors want to be helpful. Most of all they want the company to succeed – after all, it is why they invested in the first place – so the ask addresses both those things, and reinforces the feeling that both investors and entrepreneurs are still pulling in the same direction.

❯ It takes hard work on both sides to get to the point where the Board is up and functioning efficiently. At the same time, the company will be going through the growing pains of every start-up, which is what we're going to look at in the next chapter.

INVESTED INVESTOR TAKEAWAY

- The Board is there to guide and advise. It is also there to provide monitoring, governance and control.
- The Board is composed of representatives from the investors and the founders, and will include an investor director.
- Board observers do not have a vote, but are expected to contribute.
- Board packs are essential, even though they may seem time-consuming to founders of start-up companies.
- The Board, and particularly the investor director, are responsible for keeping all investors informed.
- Regular, minuted Board meetings can form essential collateral when negotiating later funding rounds or an exit.

AN ENTREPRENEUR'S STORY:
Sometimes recruiting the Board members you want takes persistence

Persuading investor Jonathan Milner to join the Board of Syndicate Room took some doing.

Jonathan had helped rescue the company when it had only two days' money left and an investment round fell through – but only on the proviso that he wouldn't be involved, since he was far too busy as CEO of his own company, Abcam; besides, Syndicate Room didn't really fit his own investment criteria.

Nevertheless, founder Gonçalo de Vasconcelos knew Jonathan and respected his advice, particularly as Jonathan had experience of scaling up and could be a valuable mentor. It started with emails, Gonçalo mentioning a challenge he was facing and asking if Jonathan had any tips, and soon they were meeting for coffee and a chat every couple of months. After a while, the coffee chats were happening every month, and then every two weeks, as Jonathan got more and more interested in the business and how it was progressing. Gonçalo now had an engaged – and much appreciated – mentor.

Eventually, Jonathan stepped down from his CEO role at Abcam and had a bit more time to spare – and now Gonçalo's persistence paid off. Jonathan joined the Board of Syndicate Room and continues to provide the team with his invaluable advice and expertise as the company grows.

CHAPTER 8

Growing pains

You've signed the shareholders' agreement and handed over your money – now what? Do you sit back and wait for your return, or can you help? If, like many invested investors, you started out as an entrepreneur yourself, your experience could be very useful; but whether or not your founders listen to you hinges on the relationship you've built up since meeting them and going through due diligence.

Baby steps

The first steps for a start-up are to build the team, prove the technology and prove the market by finding some early customers. As an invested investor, you will want to help as much as you can, because naturally you want to see the company succeed. However, if you are not an investor director, you may feel rather distant and unsure about what you can do. This is where the importance of building good relationships with your founders comes in.

I know investors who say, 'Don't go into business with people you wouldn't want to spend time with if you weren't in business with them'. That's perhaps a slightly convoluted way of saying make friends with your entrepreneurs. I call it the 'pint of beer' test – if I wouldn't want to spend time with them outside business, after a while I might not want to spend any time with them at all.

Setting up a company with your best friend is fraught with difficulty, but becoming friends with your founders is part of wanting to enjoy working with someone. And think about it – if you're investing in a particular sector, there may well be potential for mutual benefits between companies in your portfolio, and I find the best way of bringing those to light is the low-pressure scenario of a relaxed social occasion. I've seen time and time again the benefit of bringing founders together for a barbecue or other event where they can mingle and swap war stories and ideas with no agenda other than mutual sharing. Mind you, it's important not to go too far the other way. Don't go native; you'll still have to be tough at times, and you need to keep an independent perspective, otherwise you may lose the trust of the other shareholders (especially if you represent them on the Board).

> 'Most founders won't remember which investors put in the most money in the early stages, but they will remember which investors were the most helpful as they built the business.'
> Richard Lucas, serial entrepreneur and investor

If your founders appreciate not only your money but also your wisdom and experience, then they may come to you for advice when they need help with difficult decisions, or simply a confidence boost to reassure them that they're doing well. So it's important to understand some of the potential early problems for a start-up. If you've come to angel investing from a corporate career, these may be issues that you've never really had to face – hence, again, the benefit of co-investing with angels who have also been entrepreneurs – but you may still have experience that can be useful. An accounting or HR background, for instance, could be very helpful to inexperienced entrepreneurs who have never run a business before. Use your skills when and where appropriate.

Let's look at the early challenges for a start-up – the team, the technology and traction. Without them, you'll never get to the fourth T, treasure (profitability or exit).

Building the team

Once a start-up has its first investment, building the team is essential – with two founders (my ideal, one technical and one commercial), there's no way they will be able to do everything between them. A technology start-up will find itself developing the technology and building the team simultaneously – exciting times, but also very stressful times, as they have to get both right.

When I interviewed him for a podcast, Simon Thorpe shared that the main factor for one of his most successful investments to date, SwiftKey, was how good the founders were at building a superbly skilled and highly coherent team. In fact, the SwiftKey exit was more about the team than about the technology. The company was founded by Jon Reynolds and Ben Medlock in 2008 (Chris Hill-Scott was with them briefly at the beginning, but left after two months). By the time SwiftKey was acquired by Microsoft for a reported $250 million in 2016, Reynolds and Medlock had grown the team to 160 people. Going from two to 160 people in eight years is pretty fast growth, but the founders made an excellent job of hiring the right people, mostly very talented engineers, and that is what made SwiftKey so attractive to Microsoft (we'll talk about the benefits of strategic acquisitions, which this was, in Chapter 10).

Another fellow investor, Simon King, reckons that one of the biggest problems for growing companies after an A round of investment is when the CEO has to hand over to a sales team. In the early days, when the company can't afford a separate sales function, it's typically the CEO who takes the product out into the world. The CEO knows everything about it and can sell it to anyone, as they know intimately what problems the product solves. But the sales won't have been productised, won't have been broken down into a step-by-step, repeatable process. Bringing in new hires to build a sales team is almost inevitably associated with a dip in sales as they get up to speed on what they're selling and to whom. Hence this is a key moment for the young company, and where your contacts in particular could be very important in finding the right person.

Do you have to keep the team together in the same place? I've been involved with two companies where the founder CEO has moved overseas but remained with the company. One went to Brazil for several years, worked remotely and maintained contacts by visiting the UK twice a year. The other went to New York but the company had an office there anyway, so he was still part of the operation. Neither company suffered as a result. Today, it's becoming much more common for people to work remotely and younger generations are coming through for whom remote working is the norm. I know I say I don't make investments if companies are too far away for me to visit them easily, because I'm a great believer in face-to-face contact, but sometimes you have to go with what works best for the founders and senior team.

I've recently been introduced to a company that claimed to have a tool that will analyse whether the team will work well together under a variety of stresses – are they the perfect team? I'm not convinced – I think gut instinct has a key role to play – but I'm also aware that gut instincts might lead you astray, particularly when it comes to building a diverse team.

Ensuring that your founders don't just hire 'people like us' is crucial. There are numerous studies demonstrating that diverse teams are more creative, innovate more, make fewer herding mistakes and are ultimately more successful that less diverse teams. But people still tend to hire in their own likeness. This was recently illustrated for me when I interviewed an entrepreneur for one of the podcasts on the Invested Investor website. The founders and the whole team had PhDs. The company failed and this lack of diversity was given as one of the reasons.

Classic research studies, such as using identical CVs but switching between male and female names, have long demonstrated that there are conscious and unconscious biases at play in recruitment. Blind auditions for orchestras were introduced in the 1970s and 1980s, and proved a successful way to reduce gender bias, but it's not so easy to replicate that method in the world of technology start-ups. Nevertheless, you should do what you can to help your founders keep diversity at the forefront when hiring new employees.

Lack of diversity is not an option. Mark Suster, founder of Upfront Ventures, recently shared his approach to diversity on Twitter.

> 'So I submitted a term sheet this week for a seed deal with our "VC Inclusion Clause" in it and a lawyer had the gumption to try and water it down. I politely asked the founder to switch law firms.'

He also shared the inclusion clause his company includes in its term sheet:

> 'Upfront Ventures strives to invest in companies that are consciously working to create a diverse leadership team – one that's inclusive across gender, ethnicity, age, sexual orientation, disabilities and national origins. While we would never impose hiring decisions, we aim to reduce the potential impact of unconscious bias for key C-Level and senior roles within a company. We therefore ask that each portfolio company include an "inclusion rule" in its HR policies so that at least one woman and/or member of a population currently underrepresented within the company shall be formally interviewed for any open executive position.'

And the lawyer's watered-down version of this clause? 'The company agrees to use commercially reasonable efforts to build a diverse leadership team.'

Proving the technology

Sometimes, a company needs very early investment to prove the concept, before the founders can start pitching for seed money. More typically, the founders will have gone at least some way to proving their technology and have started working with potential customers to refine it. The minimum viable product (MVP) is usable, but not necessarily saleable. The team can get others to use it without being too embarrassed at its performance – such as beta software, which may still have a few bugs and can't be sold as if it's the final product.

The traditional assumption with technology start-ups is that they need to patent something, anything, even. You may find you have to curb your founders' enthusiasm for patenting everything in sight; sometimes it simply isn't sensible, useful or affordable.

Patents can be expensive to defend – their only value might be if you sue infringers and win. But a small company will almost never stand a chance against an industry giant, because they simply won't have the resources to pursue the case to a satisfactory end result.

On the other hand, patents might be key to the business model. If the plan is to license the technology, then it needs to be protected. Another important reason for taking out patents is to make the company more attractive – and therefore worth a higher price – as an acquisition. You might find that the best option is to recommend the founders operate in stealth mode for a while, and then file for patents when the technology is more robust.

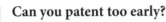 **Can you patent too early?**
'We filed two patents at the end of 2013, but they were worthless two years later because our own technology was already so much better.'

Alex Schey, Vantage Power

Finding customers

'The only money that really matters in the long run in a business is the money that comes from customers.'

Richard Lucas, serial entrepreneur and investor

Part of the original due diligence will involve understanding the business model and, most importantly, how it will make money. But making money and hopefully eventually becoming profitable won't happen right away; the company will have to find its customers, perhaps even build a community (although that's not relevant to most of my investments, it is to many consumer and platform businesses).

Plenty of pitches point to companies like Facebook and Instagram, where it wasn't evident at the outset how they were going to monetise the business, and claim that their business will follow a similar trajectory. 'We'll build a thing, people will love it, and hey presto.' But countless other businesses started with similarly vague ideas about how they might make money in the future and never lasted the distance – Facebook and Instagram are exceptions rather than the rule.

For the angel investor, I think it is imperative to understand how a business will make money, even if the thinking is as basic as 'This product will cost us X to make and we'll sell it for 5X'. If that's a realistic equation, given the underlying data, then the business should work, provided the cost of acquiring a customer is much less than 4X. Investor Richard Lucas turned down an entrepreneur who hadn't identified any potential clients. The founder said, 'I'm really convinced it's a good idea.' Richard says, 'The client's opinion is the only one that really matters, far more important than both the entrepreneur's and the investor's assessment of the product or service.' It's not about the entrepreneur's opinion – if they claim that thousands or millions of people will want their product, then surely they can find a few to demonstrate its desirability?

Can you help the business find its customers? In B2B, where I'm most comfortable, connections and networks can be key to getting a foot in the door. As an investor you can certainly help with introductions to the people that matter and hope that the team takes advantage of the opportunity. If all, or most, of your investments are in a sector you know, you might even find that some of the companies in your portfolio can work together and find unexpected synergies.

Making introductions is just the first step. In B2B, where the sales value may be a large amount of money, decisions are not taken quickly, however compelling the proposition. Generally, you can expect B2B selling to be at least a six-month proposition, because the customer will have to do due diligence on your company, and if the technology is highly innovative, it will have to be explained. One start-up I know spent almost a year describing its concept to customers, and getting the first customer to sign up was key to unlocking funding for initial trials.

This lengthy selling process is one reason why invested investors know that the milestones and targets in the original business plan are unlikely to be met. Founders who are starting their first business will probably not have any comparable experience, even if they have worked in the sector in other roles, and will have over-optimistic ideas about timings. It will take longer than they expect to make the first significant sales, just as it will take longer than they expect to build the right team to deliver on those sales.

Helping the company find customers outside the UK might also be somewhere you can help, again with introductions and an understanding of the different issues involved in selling overseas. Most UK businesses want to break into the US, and many try too early, spend too much money and then have to retrench when it doesn't work out. If this is your area of experience, you can add a lot of value and help the company explore expansion abroad in a realistic and pragmatic way.

You can also advise when it looks as if the company is too reliant on one or a few customers for the bulk of its revenues. Losing a big customer can be not only a blow to revenues, but can also put potential investors off if it comes just before a funding round. A big drop in sales raises the burn rate so existing funds won't last as long, and the company needs to put a plan in place rapidly to compensate for the lost revenues – which could even involve selling to another department within the same customer. I invested in an established business pre-IPO, not my usual modus operandi, but I knew and respected the founder and the Board. It has been an excellent investment but 97% of the company's sales were to one, albeit huge, customer. Now, they have literally millions of small customers – a major and very successful pivot.

Changes at the top

It is a truth universally acknowledged that a start-up with funds and poised to grow to the next level is in need of an experienced CEO. It is not that common for a founder-entrepreneur to lead their company all the way from start-up to a big exit and beyond. Bill Gates is Bill Gates because he is an exception. Steve Jobs was kicked out of his own company in 1985 because the Board and shareholders thought he was trying to take Apple in the wrong direction. Although Jobs came back more than a decade later and made Apple into a world-beater, the Board may well have been right at the time.

This is a crucial moment for any start-up, and the founder who takes on the role of CEO needs to understand from the outset that it is unlikely that they will still be CEO when the company exits or goes through an IPO. That said, it is always possible that they are one of those exceptional people who can go all the way, so the invested investor should do everything they can to help the founder CEO learn and develop themselves as they develop the company.

Since it is far more common for the founder-CEO to be replaced at these critical points, the options are that the founder-CEO moves aside to allow someone more experienced at leading a growing company to step in, or, in the more difficult cases, leaves altogether, which can be very painful and emotional for all involved. A founder may have to leave for entirely different reasons, such as illness, but this happens rarely.

Technology entrepreneurs are frequently focused on the technology. They set up companies to share their brilliant ideas with the world, not to grow their skills as a manager. Combining the CEO and technology roles is all very well when the company is small and the team is working 24/7 to get their product right for the market, but there are stages in a company's growth, typically reflected in the number of employees, where different skills are needed. Managing ten people in a small office where everyone knows what everyone else is working on is one thing; managing 100 people across two or more continents is a different proposition.

The solution is often to suggest that the founder switches to a different role that plays to their strengths, for instance becoming Chief Technology Officer, or Chief Product Officer. Both sides need to understand the reasons for the change and accept them, otherwise there will be problems when the new CEO comes in.

Many CEO-founders find it hard to accept that they cannot do the job once the company gets past a certain stage. Ego and pride can get in the way of making a decision that is best for the company and the investors, and things can start to go wrong. Or they can't bring themselves to stay with the company if they're not going to be CEO, and leave with bad feelings all round. Conversely, it can also be a very positive experience for the company when the founder-CEO moves willingly into a new role, because they help to keep the original vision alive and their knowledge and skills aren't lost to the business.

Some CEO-founders do understand, and know when to ask for help, and when they need coaching (as opposed to mentoring) – and those are some of the characteristics you should have been looking for during due diligence.

Investors may also use a new funding round as a bargaining chip to make changes in senior management, and this often happens when professional VC money comes in, because the VCs will have strong opinions about who will be best to protect and grow their investment. That's usually a new CEO with proven experience of growing a start-up through the series funding stages, where much more money is involved and much more is at stake.

Founders who step aside to make way for a more experienced CEO are also protecting their own investment. They have shares in the company and may well have put some of their own money in, as well as their time and expertise, so they, too, will want a return at some point; commonly 95%-plus of their wealth is tied up in their own company. If they don't understand that what is best for the company is also best for their bank balance, then there are problems.

Whatever the reason for the changes, the difficult conversations between the founder and the Board are inevitably followed by difficult conversations with the rest of the team. Are they willing to carry on without the figurehead? Was the founder so inspiring that the team will be demoralised and the company might go into the doldrums? Can the rest of senior management, the Board and the other shareholders keep the vision alive?

Ultimately, who makes a founder leave? The Board may be first to notice that things aren't working but I've found that, more than half the time, it's actually one of the founders who loses motivation and no longer believes that remaining in the business is right for them. This is a personal decision that they may well have struggled with, and you have to respect it, however difficult it makes life for the company.

One of the co-founders in a company I was involved in decided, quite correctly, that they weren't needed any more. The company had spent nine months trying to identify what product to sell, and since the co-founder was supposed to be selling the product but had nothing to sell yet, he felt no reason to stay. We had to negotiate his departure and buying out his shareholding, which was difficult, as we had very little data on which to work out a reasonable price at that stage, but it was all amicable, since he had made the decision. Conveniently, he went on to start another company that became the first company's biggest customer for a while – and helped them discover what product they should be developing and selling, which led to a good exit, a very neat result.

Another time, and less amicably, I had a company in my portfolio where the CEO fell out with one of the co-founders. I spent a long time trying to repair things, which led to a compromise that ultimately didn't work, and so the co-founder left anyway. And finally, I've seen a co-founder leave because the company had morphed into a business that he no longer wanted to build. Since success in business is so dependent on the people involved, you have to respect their decisions when they have a change of heart.

Once you know a founder is leaving, the Board has to look at the options for dealing with the issue. Although I recommend transparency at all times, this is another of the few occasions where it would almost certainly be incorrect to involve the investors until the outcome is clear. It will be up to the Board in their conversations with the founder to determine how complicated the situation might become, and, if possible, present the rest of the investors with the solution once everything has been ironed out. One reason for this is that one or more of the shareholders might be particularly closely involved with the founder (especially if they are family, or have invested in the founder's previous start-ups) and they might muddy the waters in what could be complicated negotiations. This is where the good leaver/bad leaver provisions included in the legal documents (see Chapter 6) prove their worth.

> One reason founders sometimes leave is because the company has to pivot in order to survive. The pivot is a frequent scenario in start-ups, so that's what Chapter 9 is all about.

> **INVESTED INVESTOR TAKEAWAY**
> - Building the team is a key early activity, and you can help with suggestions and by encouraging diversity.
> - Proving the technology or concept can take time and possibly more money.

- Proving the market may require your help with contacts and introductions.
- Founder-CEOs rarely stay in position all the way through to exit. Do your best to help them grow with the role, but be prepared to have difficult conversations.

AN ENTREPRENEUR'S STORY:
The accidental launch

I didn't understand the original premise for Rapportive, Martin Kleppmann's idea for a browser add-on. Rapportive set out to help professionals establish better rapport with their contacts. Previously, if you wanted to know who was signing up to a service or product by email, you would have to check LinkedIn and other social media sites separately to build up a picture so that you could tailor your response. Martin, along with colleagues Rahul and Sam, had created a tool that made this much simpler – they saw it as a 'head-up display' for the web – and meant that responses to individual emailers could be more nuanced and appropriate.

Then things went a little crazy. Martin and his team decided to see if their idea was of interest to the internationally known seed accelerator Y Combinator, and began the application process. As part of the application, the team put up a website explaining what Rapportive did and offering a free download.

All very reasonable, but the website was not password protected, and a friend of Kleppmann's sent a link to a blogger they knew. The blogger tried Rapportive, was very excited by it, and wrote about it. Other bloggers picked it up, some with large numbers of readers, and within 24 hours there were 10,000 users of something Kleppmann hadn't planned to launch just yet.

Martin was still in the earn-out phase after selling his first company to Redgate Software, so he was still contractually obliged to them and had to have an awkward conversation about how he'd just started something accidentally and it was going really well. Luckily, he had a very good relationship with Redgate, and they gave him their blessing to switch his attention to Rapportive.

Y Combinator's strategy is to select companies, bring the team to Silicon Valley for three months where they would provide them with advice and introductions, and take a 7% stake in the company for $20,000 in seed money. By the end of the three months, the companies are ready to pitch to a room full of investors at Demo Day in order to obtain the funding they'll need to carry on and build.

But now the team was having a different conversation with Y Combinator – they needed to raise money quickly to take advantage of the momentum and excitement that was building up, and did not wait until after they had gone through the three-month programme. Essentially, Martin was in the driving seat, and told them that if they were interested in investing on their usual terms, they would have to move fast.

The vast majority of companies selected by Y Combinator travel to their HQ in Silicon Valley to pitch and go through an intense selection process. The Rapportive team was interviewed over Skype and the investment was sealed over the phone.

Rapportive ended up raising about $1 million in seed money altogether but it was almost all spent on salaries. The type of work visa that the team had to obtain to move to Silicon Valley specified that they had to be paid at market rates, which was much more than they'd have been paid (or expected) in the UK and, of course, the staff they hired in the US also expected the same rates.

Nevertheless, Rapportive had a growing user base, and they were adding the sort of features that they wanted for themselves. It was still free, and revenues still seemed distant. But with revenues in mind, the team started working on ideas for premium features that they could charge for, and a subscription service for business users who could use Rapportive to link their customer relationship management systems with email and social media.

Since the seed money was going to run out within two years, Rapportive got working on a series A funding round pretty quickly. By now, the number of active users was around 200,000, but it turned out that even though that sounds like a lot it wasn't enough to get VCs interested. One million users might have been enough.

What to do? They had quite a large group of angel investors, and could have gone to them for more money to keep Rapportive going until it was big enough for series A. There was no formal Board – things are different in the US – and communications with shareholders were somewhat ad hoc. The premium product was nearly ready to launch but they had no idea whether it would be successful or not. Silicon Valley is very keen on visions, so they could have gone to investors and sold the vision even if the premium product hadn't proved itself.

But in the meantime, a conversation had started with LinkedIn. The team resolved that if LinkedIn did not acquire them, they would go back to the angels and keep growing the company, but eventually things got serious and the acquisition process began.

Martin points out that bringing in an experienced mergers and acquisitions (M&A) broker to help them with the deal was crucial, and the broker was totally fair and more than earned their fee. Among the elements under negotiation were price, cash vs stock ratios, how to structure deals for employees who owned few shares but had made major contributions, and a vesting schedule. After the acquisition, the team joined LinkedIn and continued to develop what would be launched 18 months later as LinkedIn Intro.

CHAPTER 9

The pivot

The original business plan is typically based on incomplete knowledge and evolves over time – so what happens when you and your founders realise that it isn't going to work after all? If the basic idea and the team are still good, perhaps it's time to pivot.

What is a pivot?

As the name suggests, a pivot is when a company changes its direction and its fundamental offering. The *Financial Times* describes pivots in terms of 'the tortured path that most start-ups go through to find the right customer, value proposition, and positioning'. Pivots occur when something happens to stop the original business plan from continuing, and should be driven by new knowledge about customers, the technology and/or the market.

Businesses are set up to treat pain points for their eventual customers but the founders won't have had time to do a lot of in-depth market research, and before they get the company off the ground, they probably won't have spent many hours with end users. So, inevitably, the business plan you invest into is incomplete and subject to change as the founders learn more about the ecosystem and what potential customers need.

> 'It's a mistake to keep trying [with the same idea] and assume that you'll get there in the end. That's bollocks. The most important thing is to listen to the market, understand what your customers are telling you and what their activity is telling you, so you can keep iterating the business until you find what works. Even the best businesses have been through multiple iterations.'
> Simon Murdoch, Episode 1 Ventures

A pivot may be necessary because the business model is not working, but the founders and investors still believe in the original premise and the team. Or it may be an opportunity to grow into an area that wasn't obvious – or even in existence – when the team started out. The underlying core idea probably remains, just the direction it should go in needs to change. You can think of it like ultimate frisbee, where the player holding the frisbee can't travel, but can rotate 360 degrees on the spot, pivoting around on one leg while they look for the next pass.

Among the 14 famous business pivots mentioned in a 2013 *Forbes* article are Twitter, which, believe it or not, started out as a podcast subscription service called Odeo; Starbucks, which went from selling coffee beans and espresso makers to selling cups of coffee (and didn't that scale?); and Nokia, which started out as a paper mill in Finland. Some pivots are extreme, like Nokia getting from paper to mobile phones, whereas others are more evolutionary, such as Starbucks.

Since many early stage businesses find they have to pivot at some point in their development, it's important to assess the founders' attitudes to learning and change before you invest. Founders who are too stubborn to listen to advice and act on it can bring everything to a juddering halt.

> **6** 'Don't invest if your reason for following on includes requiring founders or the executive team to change their behaviour. It is very hard to change behaviour. If they're totally on board and keen to change, that's ok, but if they're reluctant, it won't work.'
>
> Andy Phillipps, entrepreneur and investor

A good founder will spot that the market is not keen on their product and admit it, and will work through the issue with the Board. They will understand the need to pivot, and recognise that pivoting will probably need more investment. They will also understand the

need to get everybody on the team to buy in to the new direction, essential if the pivot is going to be successful.

The Board may spot when a pivot is needed before the founders do – and if the founders are first-time entrepreneurs, they may not expect to pivot at all. If the founders are unwilling to change the business model or product, the company will fail. If they agree to pivot but don't buy in 100%, they'll do it half-heartedly and the company will fail unless drastic action is taken.

Pivots are expensive and difficult – they will almost certainly require more investment and a modified vision. It's not always easy to spot the right pivot, and companies with patient and faithful investors may change direction more than once before they get it right.

> **6**   'Find out all you can early and adjust course while you still can – investors are more sympathetic to change than to running out of time.'
>
> Gordon MacSween, entrepreneur

Shareholders generally support a pivot when it becomes necessary – invested investors understand that change is an inevitable part of growing a young business. Indeed, they may be even more enthusiastic about the new direction than they were about the original business plan.

The technology pivot

Sometimes the technology just doesn't work. But it might be possible to change it and still create a business around it, or a new technology can be licensed in. For instance, one company was founded to commercialise IP in a novel material that they hoped could be used to address the significant problem of hospital-acquired infections, particularly those related to the use of urinary catheters. They believed that their material could be used to coat the catheters and prevent the build-up of bacterial biofilms, the route of most infections. Unfortunately, adhesion was a problem, so they licensed in IP from another source, which helped them get round this problem.

A technology business that is still trying to get its product right might take contract work in the meantime to keep it afloat, which also gives it valuable insights into what the pain points are for customers.

Sometimes, a technology pivot is more about how – and to whom – you sell the product. Martin Kleppmann's first company, Go Test It, was aimed at solving a problem for website developers. Go Test It was a hosted service that could analyse how a website behaved on different browsers to make sure it was fully functional across all of them. But using Go Test It required training and it was difficult to persuade website developers to incorporate it into their workflow as a hosted service. Since it looked like Go Test It was never going to be a commercial proposition, Martin was thinking of giving up and going back to university to do a PhD. But in a serendipitous moment, local company Redgate Software invited

Martin and his team to move into their offices, because they had taken on premises that were too big for them. Moving into the Redgate office gave Martin the chance to meet other developers and start to think about his product in a different way, especially as he was encouraged to spend more time talking to potential users and gained a clearer understanding of how the product might fit into their workflow and their business. Redgate also got to know Martin's team and the technology. Since Redgate were in the developer tool business, they saw the Go Test It product as a good fit and ultimately acquired Martin's company. Although in the end Go Test It didn't go anywhere, a very similar product using very similar technology – including some of Go Test It's technology – is still going strong.

The market-driven pivot

Young businesses can be stymied by the competition. They may find they can't get into the market because it would mean competing solely on price rather than the differentiator of their technology.

Never compete on price if you want to scale a business. Small businesses by their nature have to keep a very careful eye on cash flow and profitability, and don't have much room for manoeuvre when it comes to pricing.

Sometimes even Uber can't compete. March 2018 saw Uber announce that it was exiting the Southeast Asia market, folding its existing business there into competitor ride-hailing business Grab. Having at one time sought global market dominance, this was the latest retraction for Uber, after China and Russia also proved too hard to crack.

The most likely reason to pivot is lack of market. If customers don't want the product at all, it has to be changed. Or the product might be adored, but only by a few customers. Or, most commonly, only early adopter customers will pay enough to generate a scalable business. In any case, there aren't the sales to grow the business.

One company I'm involved in had a very good product but only a small market. It was highly defensible but the sales volumes were not there. So they took the risk of developing a new product that was less defensible, although it still used some of the IP from the original product, and launching it into a much larger market. The risk of lower defensibility was offset by the attraction of the market, and ratcheting up revenues would help them keep their core technology ahead of the competition.

Another market-driven pivot comes about when the regulatory environment changes. New rules can come in that force a company to change direction. Sometimes these new rules are heralded well in advance, and there is plenty of time to assess how best to accommodate them. But sometimes things move fast and a company has to be nimble to keep up. For instance, the European emissions standards (Euro 1–6) for diesel engines cut permissible nitrous oxide (NOx) levels by more than half between Euro 5 (2009) and Euro 6 (2014). One of my portfolio companies was founded to retrofit diesel engines to meet the Euro 5 regime, and had to pivot their focus to Euro 6 and revisit their technology when the new regulations came in.

As an invested investor, you can help your portfolio companies by watching what is going on in the broader environment and picking up on changes that might pose problems for them, or indeed in some cases offer opportunities. The founders are likely to be extremely busy with the day-to-day dramas of growing a new business, and taken up by the minutiae, particularly building and managing teams, so they have little time to look at the big picture.

The service-to-product pivot

You can have a perfectly decent service business with a few employees, but it won't scale to give the kind of return an invested investor needs. Service businesses can only grow by employing more people; they can't be scaled in the same way as a product business.

When you offer a service, you adapt it to help individual customers solve their particular problems. If you have more employees, you can help more customers, but growth is about hiring and training people to deliver the service, and necessarily slow.

A product business means you are offering something that doesn't change to suit each customer – once you have found what customers want, you can make more of it and sell it to more customers.

That said, plenty of companies have started out offering a service before they have developed, or even chosen, what product they're going to offer. The service helps them to generate income in the early days, bootstrapping the business until they are ready for investment. Typically, this type of business will find the right product through projects with customers; they will get to know the pain points for their customers and also identify where there are gaps in the market that they can fill. They might work with customers to develop the product, or they might work on it at nights and weekends in stealth mode, but all the time they will be learning more about their potential market and customers.

The distinction isn't always clear – but a key warning signal for invested investors is a pitch that doesn't distinguish between the two at all. Selling services requires very different sales skills from selling products, and I won't invest where the founders claim they can do both without good evidence that what they say is true. Besides, starting out with a foot in both camps will result in split loyalties – will the founders spend enough time developing their product, or will they be focused on generating income through the consultancy side?

When is a product business not a product business? At Camdata, we had an industrial electronics product called Atlas – named for the rugged mountain range because a key differentiator was its strength and durability. Atlas was launched as a series with nine variants, but we rarely sold any as standard products. In reality, the Atlas was a demonstration of our capability in solving durability problems, but then we were functioning as a service (in this case customising the hardware and firmware) once we had our foot in the door. We weren't building hundreds or thousands of Atlas terminals, we were adapting them each time to fit, so it never became a true product business. A proper business, but not one that scaled well, nor one that could raise equity, although we did try.

A very successful product business, Domino Printing, was spun out of a service business, Cambridge Consultants, back in the late 1970s. Cambridge Consultants wasn't going to pivot and focus entirely on inkjet printing, because it offered a huge range of technology services to its customers and breadth was as important as depth to its own growth. The answer was to spin Domino out and let it become a product business in its own right, which it achieved in stellar fashion, forming the core of one of the most successful inkjet printing clusters in the world and eventually being acquired by Brother for over £1 billion in 2015.

Very rarely, the pivot can go the other way – I'm a very invested investor in a company called James and James Fulfilment. It started out as a pure technology company, developing software that helped run a warehouse to fulfil customer orders. The founders then developed a service business around the software to test it and that started to take off. Now, although the founders have monetised their technology by selling it on to others in the value chain, it accounts for only 0.3% of revenue and 0.6% of profit. Alongside that, they have developed a large service business based on excellent core technology.

The cost of pivoting
One of the key points about a pivot is that the company will almost certainly need more investment in order to make the change. Any change in direction or product can be expensive. There are financial costs and people costs, and pivots should not be undertaken lightly.

If the pivot is well thought-through and costed as accurately as possible, it is very unusual for none of the existing shareholders to follow on and put in more money. The original due diligence holds, the team is still investible, the company just needs more time to find the sweet spot. Invested investors understand that this is par for the course and won't be surprised.

If too few shareholders follow on, and those that remain don't put up all the funds required, the change in direction and business plan has to be good enough to attract new investors, and this is where things might get more difficult.

Shareholders might not follow on for various reasons, some to do with the finances, and some to do with their portfolio and their investment criteria. Sometimes angels don't follow on because the new valuation is out of proportion and they see the risk as too high to invest further. If the pivot takes the company into a sector that is unfamiliar to the investors, they might feel that their cash is better directed to where they can contribute more value to a start-up. They will probably also feel that the company itself will be better served by investors who bring the different knowledge and contacts that support its new direction.

When shareholders don't follow on, the management will need time to identify and woo new investors, and one of the issues they'll have to address is why shareholders haven't followed on.

TRANSPARENCY TAKEAWAY

If potential new investors see that shareholders are not following on for personal or pragmatic reasons rather than because they don't have faith in the company, they will be more inclined to listen favourably to an investment pitch.

A pivot might be the time to bring in venture capital. This changes everything. If the Board agrees that this is necessary, they will want to choose the VCs they'll partner with very carefully. Venture capital not only brings larger sums, now and later on; it can also come with essential experience that might be key to making the pivot successful. VCs are also generally better at keeping an eye on the big picture, because investing and supporting growing businesses is their day job – whereas many angel investors do their investing in their spare time. But VC money can also bring different ways of working, so investors and founders need to be aware that things may change, and that can be a challenge. There's more on what happens when it's time for VC investment in Chapter 5.

There might also be a personal cost to a pivot, such as the loss of one of the founders if they don't agree with the new plan. This can be beneficial, or it can make life very difficult. It is hard to force a founder out of a company if they are reluctant to pivot, but it can be even harder to convince a founder to stay if they have lost belief.

> Pivoting can be a key moment on the road to an exit, something every invested investor wants to reach. Some exits are successful and provide large returns, and we'll look at those in the next chapter.

INVESTED INVESTOR TAKEAWAY

- A pivot is not a sign of failure – many, if not most, businesses pivot on their way to optimising the model.
- Pivots can be driven by a number of factors, including the technology, the market and the business model.
- Founders and investors should be aware when a pivot becomes necessary.
- Pivots may require additional funding.

AN ENTREPRENEUR'S STORY:
If at first you don't succeed – pivot, and pivot and pivot again

The vision behind William Tunstall-Pedoe's company True Knowledge was to be able to answer any question, in any language, in one second or less. The key differentiator for the technology was how it worked with natural language so that the answer came up straight away, rather than the typical experience of being given a list of possible answers and having to browse through them to find the right one. A pioneer of structured data and conversational search, it took the company several pivots to reach the right business model, but when they did, they soon had a string of suitors knocking on their door.

The first business model was to build a website, trueknowledge. com, that would answer questions posed in natural language. William and two colleagues in a cramped office managed to put together a crude demo and secure £650,000 in angel funding in 2007. The first VC round came in 2008, with Octopus Ventures putting in around £2 million.

The website competed with Google (back in the days when that was not considered a totally crazy thing to do). A database of facts was built up, and the natural language algorithms meant that users could ask questions that other search engines could not answer. For instance, 'Is Madonna single?' confused search engines that could not distinguish between a relationship and a music single. The True Knowledge site could also answer the question, 'What time is it at Google HQ?', which left Google stumped.

But a geeky, badly designed website was ultimately no match for Google and the like, so the company had to pivot to survive.

Business model number two was to license the technology to the bigger search companies, Google, Bing, Yahoo, Yandex (Russia), Baidu (China) and so on. Negotiations with one of these companies went on for two years, but ended nowhere. Some smaller deals were not enough to convince the team and the investors that things were working, so it was time for another change.

Model number three was built around getting content into searches by having it indexed, a version of search engine optimisation, which directed traffic to trueknowledge.com. Visits to the site started to grow rapidly, at over 10% per week for almost all of 2010. In September of that year, they recorded 3.8 million visits, then 4.4 million in October and 5.2 million in November. December visits came to 5.8 million and the peak in January 2011 was 7.2 million.

The plan was to monetise through advertising, and for a while this worked. A major PR coup was when True Knowledge revealed the most boring day in the history of the world – 11 April 1954 – which continues to hit the headlines every April. But the next financing round failed just when they needed extra funding to keep up with and capitalise on their growth. To make matters worse, Google changed its algorithm in February 2011, taking a big chunk of True Knowledge's traffic and convincing the team that they were on the wrong path.

The team went into lockdown to deliver the next pivot – their own, branded mobile product for a voice assistant. Apple launched Siri in October 2011, True Knowledge launched their own voice software, christened Evi, in January 2012.

Evi received a lot of positive press, and was downloaded over one million times in the first four months after launch, becoming a top seller on iTunes in the US and the UK (even though it was competing with Apple's own offering). Finally, the company was generating significant revenue, earlier than expected but most welcome.

William and the investors had been talking about the need for a different kind of CEO to deal with the new challenges and in April 2012, Barak Berkowitz came on board to help take the company to the next stage. With 30 years' experience building tech businesses, Barak was known and respected by William, who took on the role of Chief Product Officer. The new CEO started to plan for setting up a Silicon Valley office and changed the name of the company to Evi, its now highly visible brand with over a million downloads – one every ten seconds since launch.

Evi received over 40 approaches from large companies interested in their natural language processing technology. Eventually, they received two formal offers, one of which came from Amazon, and the acquisition was finalised in late 2012, less than a year after Evi was launched. Today, Evi is better known by her new name, Alexa.

CHAPTER 10

The successful exit

Exits come in many different shapes and sizes, from the blaze of glory marked by a strategic acquisition that returns multiple times the initial investment to the damp squib of no return. Or the worst-case scenario, the insolvent failure, where it is not only the shareholders who lose money, but others as well, such as trade creditors and the government. Invested investors are pragmatic, but underneath always optimistic, so let's talk about successful exits first.

What is an exit?

The exit is where you get your money back, you hope, with a return, even better, and possibly a very good return, better still. All investments are made with a view to a future return, whether they are buying shares on a stock market or buying a buy-to-let house, and angel investing is no different. But since it is inherently far riskier than buying shares or a house, it is not an investment you can rely on to fund your later years. There are exits where you get absolutely nothing back, and occasionally exits where you receive a cheque for many times your initial investment, but most non-zero exits lie somewhere in between.

The exit doesn't necessarily mark the end of your relationship with a particular company. There could be an earn out period, or the exit could be partly or wholly funded through the acquirer's shares, which you must then decide when to sell (sometimes for a much better return than if you'd taken cash at the initial exit point). And your relationship with the founders and other investors may well continue in new start-ups and other companies.

I've been an angel investor long enough to see a few of my investments exit and learn some valuable lessons along the way. I also work with a large number of angels and entrepreneurs who have been in the game for much longer than me and seen many more exits, as well as with those who are still waiting for their first.

Exits happen in good ways and bad ways. The good exits occur when the company you have invested in is sold, floats on a stock market, or enters a formal partnership with another company that buys out the existing investors and whichever way it goes, you get a return on your investment. The not-so-good exits could be one of the above where you don't see a return, or could be the company going out of business, and we'll look at those in the next chapter.

There are also partial exits, known as secondaries. This is an opportunity for the shareholders, possibly including the founders, to sell some of their shares in a secondary sale, where a percentage of the company, that is, a certain number of shares, is permitted to be sold. One reason the founders might want to sell some of their shares is to raise some cash – this gives them a partial reward for their efforts in setting up and growing the company, and enables them to diversify, so that they don't have their entire life's worth bound up in one entity. Or they might simply want to pay off that second mortgage they took out to get the company going.

It is important to note that the cash released by secondaries should be limited so that the founders don't become demotivated. Generally, it is reasonable for the founders to be permitted to sell 10% of their total shareholding (e.g. 3% if they own 30% of the business) if they want to at this stage – but that depends on the numbers. If the company is already doing very well and that 10% is worth £10 million, the founder might simply buy the yacht they've always wanted and sail away. Context is always important.

Invested investors might also want to sell some of their shares to release cash that they can recycle back into new start-ups, and to de-risk their portfolio. Often, the shares are sold to a VC or private equity company that wants to buy in, and it will be the buying organisation that sets the price. The VC or other buyer will want to buy a certain percentage of the company, so the deal is dependent on enough shareholders being willing to sell enough shares to meet the VC's requirement.

> Secondaries can be very good for invested investors if they come at the right time and at the right price. A private equity house bought out the angels who had funded pet nutraceuticals company Lintbells, giving them a large multiple on their original investment. A different company went through a round that saw all the angels bought out – but then it went into liquidation. The angels were lucky to get out while the going was good.

A typical scenario when people talk about the likelihood of a good exit starts with a portfolio of ten companies (which I've argued earlier is too small, but it's convenient for illustrative purposes here). Out of these ten companies, three will fail pretty quickly. Losing your money quickly is better than losing it agonisingly slowly – and preferably before you've put in another round, or two.

Now you've got seven companies left. Of these, perhaps five or six will trundle along doing ok, not brilliantly, but not terribly and two or three of these will fail slowly. Then, if you're lucky, the other one or two companies will be doing very well and you'll be looking forward to a good exit from at least one of them. But this is all on paper – you haven't had any returns yet, and you've already lost on the three that have failed. As always, it's a numbers game, and this scenario presupposes that you've got the typical ten companies – if you make bad investment decisions or have a run of bad luck, all ten might fail.

It's worth noting that in the UK, the vast majority of exits in 2017, around 70%, were technology companies. These companies tend to grow more quickly than those in other sectors, often 30% per annum or more, which makes them attractive to potential acquirers. So I invest (mostly) in technology companies not only because that's the area I know most about, but also because it's where I'm more likely to get a good exit.

A view to an exit

The exit starts at the entrance. A good pitch will include a view of the exit. That sounds counter-intuitive – the founders are trying to persuade you to invest, but they're already predicting the disappearance of their company. Well, they're not – they're telling you how their company will get to the next level once it has grown as far as it can on angel and early stage funding.

When a company reaches the scale-up stage, it will need bigger tranches of cash, and this is where institutional investors really kick in. The point of being an angel is to get start-ups to this stage, and then exit with a decent enough return so you can start all over again with another set of founders (or even the same ones – something we'll talk about in Chapter 12).

Not everyone agrees with me that the founders need to include their vision for an exit in the pitch – in fact, some disagree strongly. But in my opinion, an invested investor cannot – should not – invest if they can't see an exit down the line, that is, some potential scenario in which they get their money back, with a positive multiple return. For me, having some mention of an exit in the pitch shows me that the founders have thought about it, and that they understand that their investors will need a return at some stage.

In fact, to put it bluntly, any company that takes angel or VC funding is for sale the very next day, that's just the way it goes. And occasionally the exit feels almost that fast – I invested in a company that exited to RightMove 18 months later, neural network company Magic Pony Technology exited to Twitter in two years, and DeepMind was acquired by Google when it was barely four years old. For the record, I didn't invest in Magic Pony or DeepMind – c'est la vie.

Those examples are unusual; things rarely happen that quickly. Views on how long it takes from investment to exit vary, but the minimum you can expect, in my experience, is around eight years. Founders will inevitably talk about exiting in three to five years, but you should know better; don't be taken in by their youthful enthusiasm.

In their pitch, the founders won't of course be predicting exactly what will happen a decade or so down the line, but you should expect them to have at least some understanding of several key factors. These include which sector or sectors potential acquirers might come from, which named companies might acquire them, possible reasons for an acquisition, where to recruit Board members who could accelerate the acquisition path, and being prepared to move fast if an opportunity presented itself unexpectedly. Let's have a look at those in a bit more detail.

Which sector or sectors do they think will be interested in them? Some start-ups are pretty niche and focus on a limited range of customers, so they might expect to be acquired by a larger company in that particular sector. Others might be targeting customers across several sectors, which obviously results in a larger pool of potential exits, but on the other hand, might mean diluting efforts across a wider range. Having an unclear exit – where there are several potential avenues to acquisition – is better than no exit vision at all.

Your founders should know their sectors and know how those sectors are growing and developing. Have they recognised a strong need in a particular area where they can create a valuable proposition? This might mean that they don't plan to monetise their product through sales, but through creating something that will give another company a competitive advantage. Building a company to address a need can be a viable investment, but there are associated risks, not least that the potential acquirers might develop their own solutions to the problem, and that plenty of other entrepreneurs might be competing to satisfy the same original need.

Who might buy them? Some start-ups decide who they hope will acquire them from the beginning and build the business accordingly. Microsoft, Google, Apple, Amazon and the other big names are constantly on the look out for technologies they can add to their offerings, and it's not unusual for a start-up to have one or more of these companies in their sights from the very early days. In Cambridge, where I'm based, several companies have been snapped up by the big guys, including Vocal IQ, which was bought by Apple to improve its Siri voice recognition software, and Evi, which was bought by Amazon for its Alexa devices.

On the other hand, I've lost count of the number of pitch decks I've seen with the Apple or Google logo included on the exit slide, with no real reason for it being there.

The founders should know that there are plenty of other companies that are keen to acquire start-ups with technologies that will help them differentiate their offerings when the right opportunity comes along. This comes back to the founders' sector knowledge, and the companies they suggest as potential acquirers will give you a good idea of how carefully they've thought about this. Of course, it may be that the eventual exit will be to a company that has still to be founded – but it's hard to develop a business plan with that in mind.

Another route to a named exit is when one or more of the founders have left their jobs with a view to creating a business that their previous employer will buy. They have contacts inside that company, and know what it's missing, or what it can't do for itself, so can be highly targeted in how they define and grow the business. This is a fairly extreme example, but it does happen. Your due diligence might need to include making sure that the founders didn't leave their previous company under a cloud and that relationships are still good, otherwise this exit route might be fraught with difficulty, and if it doesn't work, there may be nowhere else to go.

Why buy the company? Will it be be acquired for its customers, its technology or for strategic reasons? A start-up that is only a few years old is unlikely to have a very large customer base, although it may have a strong and growing foothold in a particular sector. The technology might be valuable but could face strong competition or be easily superseded. An acquirer with a strategic view on where the market is heading can identify your start-up as a key piece in taking them there, if the timing is right. Broadcom's acquisition of Element 14 took the company into the ADSL chip market, described as 'the missing piece in its broadband strategy'. As with this deal, a strategic acquisition is likely to bring the largest return to the founders and investors.

Who can help the acquisition process? Do the founders have any individuals in the industry in mind as potential non-executive directors or advisors who might be able to unlock the door to exit? You as an angel might be able to make useful introductions when the time for exit looks ripe, but usually such introductions come from contacts within the industry itself. The Board will perhaps make a strategic choice of a non-executive director, or know that they must work on building their network to increase their chances of getting face-to-face with the right people. One of my portfolio companies, Cambridge CMOS Sensors, appointed serial entrepreneur and investor Robert Swann as chairman in 2015, as it started gearing up for a further funding round in 2016. Swann also had a string of successful exits under his belt. Although unplanned in 2015, in June 2016, Cambridge CMOS Sensors was acquired by Austrian company ams AG for an undisclosed sum.

And finally, since an exit can come from anywhere – no amount of strategic planning can override serendipity – they'll need to recognise opportunities when they present themselves. One company a friend invested in found their exit at a trade show. A visitor to their stand started chatting about doing business together and within a short space of time this led to an acquisition.

> One company I know was acquired for a very large sum after an email arrived out of the blue asking if they were for sale and, if so, how much did they want? The company was still fairly new and was many years from planning an exit, so they plucked a number out of the air and asked for half a billion dollars. To their great surprise, they got it.

If there is no exit slide in the pitch deck, you will have to raise the subject yourself. I've done this more often than I'd like to, and when I see that the founders are shocked at the very mention of exit, I have to start wondering how well they understand the investor's perspective. Even though I know that any exit story at this stage is almost certainly pure fiction – how many of those companies with the Apple logo in their pitch deck ended up selling to Apple? – at least it shows that the entrepreneur is on the right page.

What's it worth?

The largest part of exit negotiations is the valuation. The Board will need to approve the valuation agreed in order to recommend it to all shareholders, which means they not only need to justify the valuation, but also to understand the appetite of their shareholders. If some of the shareholders feel the valuation is too low, they can potentially hold up or even stop the exit and nobody wins. Whatever the drivers behind the exit, you will expect your Board and advisors to achieve the best valuation for the company under the circumstances.

The sale of SwiftKey could be thought of as an ideal exit for an angel investor. The company's first funding came from the two founders, followed by a grant from Innovate UK. Two rounds of funding then came from angels, including my friend Simon Thorpe, and the next was an early VC round. A later VC round came in, with the first VCs following on, and then Microsoft came knocking on the door.

The key to SwiftKey's journey to an efficient exit was that at each round there was demonstrable commercial traction and the valuation increased accordingly, putting up the share price. The exit was split approximately in thirds between founders, angels and VCs – the angels had invested heavily in their early rounds and their shareholdings benefited from the steep rise in valuation.

The valuation should – in an ideal world – be easier when approaching an exit than in the very early stages of the journey. When you make your initial investment(s), you have relatively little concrete information to go on. By the time an exit is in the air, the company should have some indication of its commercial success, or at least a better idea of its commercial potential.

The conventional way of valuing a stable business for possible sale is to look at its earnings before interest, taxes, depreciation and amortisation (EBITDA) and multiply by three or four. But this would be regarded as very low in a scaling company, where the multiple might be six, eight or more. Essentially, EBITDA is a proxy for profitability and if, for instance, it indicates an underlying profit of £1 million, then an acquirer will probably offer £3–4 million. If the founders plan on this type of exit from the early days, they may well build the company accordingly, optimising costs to keep profits high. But this is risky, because if they can't find an exit, they may have scrimped on essentials like R&D and the company might not be in a good position to survive in the long term. This is not a conversation that technology angels want to have, as there will probably have been a decade plus to exit, and the investment multiple will be low, hence the return will be poor.

Another way of valuing a company in this situation looks at its sales to provide a multiple of revenues, since they demonstrate extent of market share and traction. However, revenues are not the same as profit, and although this method of valuation is popular, it is not particularly robust.

As an investor, your best return will come from an acquisition that is not based on EBITDA or revenues, but that happens for strategic reasons. Here, the valuation becomes far more complex because the acquirer is not necessarily looking at the profitability or otherwise of the business – a strategic acquisition is most likely to be about the technology and the team, and how much value they will add to the acquiring company. They indicate that you want your company to be bought, rather than for you to sell it, a subtle difference but one that can make all the difference to the final price.

One way of looking at it is through the understanding that you can buy people but you can't buy time. A major player might not be able to solve a problem quickly enough on its own, and an acquisition is the only way for it to keep ahead. Putting a value on that is tricky. I've seen a company acquired for around 100 times its turnover (and it was making a loss) because it was exactly what another company needed at the time. Whether or not that was a fair price may never be truly understood. The $650 million paid for Solexa by Illumina is argued to have been a steal for the US giant, bringing it the technology that has helped the company to a share of more than 75% in the global gene sequencing market.

What's your multiple?

At exit, you will get a return on the money you have invested in the company. So far, so obvious. But if you have followed on in the second and possibly third rounds, your return might not be a straightforward multiple of the original sum.

Remember my fictional company from Chapter 3, when I was talking about valuations? It's the same calculation, but now it's about your multiple. I imagined that there were 1,000 shares in a new company, and the founders kept 750 for themselves and sold 250 for £1,000 each, so the company was valued at £1 million. If there were no follow-on rounds, and the company is sold for £10 million, then the 1,000 shares are worth a total of £10 million, that is, £10,000 each or a multiple of 10X.

You're more likely to end up with a blended return at exit, so the final valuation will not necessarily indicate the multiple on your original investment. Say you bought shares for X in the first round, and when the valuation went up, you bought some more shares. By this point, your first shares might be worth 10X, but your second purchase will be at the new price. So your second set of shares at exit may only have gone up in price by 3X, and if you bought into a third round at another higher valuation, that multiple at exit might be 0.5X. Unless you have invested an identical amount in each round, your total return will not be a simple average of the different multiples – but it will still be a good return.

What happens next?

As an angel, you won't be heavily involved in the exit process unless you're on the Board. There will be another phase of due diligence

– the acquirers doing due diligence on your company, and your company doing due diligence on the acquirers. This may be when it is time to call in the advisors, but that (as with so many things) depends on circumstances.

There are three types of professional expertise that play a role during an exit: lawyers, accountants and corporate finance.

Lawyers are essential, since the exit is ultimately a legal process and needs to be robust.

You will probably want accountancy help – the acquirers will certainly be using professional accountants – although you may have someone on the Board who can perform this function.

Help from the world of corporate finance is not always essential. Although corporate financiers can often identify competitive bidders and encourage an auction to push up the price, there are reasons why you may not need, or want, their help. Corporate financiers in a £10 million plus deal will expect between £500,000 and £1,000,000 (or more) in fees, so the exit has to be worth their while – and worth your giving up that proportion of your return. If their fee is set at 5% of the final price, then the exit might have to be £20 million or above for them to feel it's worth doing. If the exit is only £5 million, then 5% of that is a mere £250,000 and they probably won't get out of bed.

Since I co-invest with other experienced investors from a wide range of backgrounds, I often find that for a smaller exit, we have sufficient expertise between us to cover everything except the legal functions.

> **Reasons to have advisors**
> - They have very good contacts and can find potential acquirers for the company – to the extent where they can make a significant difference to the size of the offer on larger deals.
> - They ensure that the information package – the prospectus – for the company is fit for purpose.

- They are independent, so can negotiate objectively during an auction (which is difficult for founders to do as there is so much emotion involved).
- They release the executive team from a lot of the work involved in preparing for an exit, allowing them to maintain their focus on running the company. This can be essential for the company's future if the exit doesn't happen.

Reasons not to have advisors

- The deal isn't big enough for them – or their fees will take too big a chunk of your return.
- There is enough skill on the Board to cover what's needed.

When there is more than one bidder, the process will include trying to decide which of the potential acquirers is the best fit for the company, and what they intend to do with it once the acquisition goes through. A multinational that wants to move the entire team to the other side of the world might be less attractive than an alternative bidder who wants to keep the team where they are and grow the company as its UK base.

It's up to the Board to make sure that all options and all bidders have been thoroughly investigated before they make their recommendation to sell or not to sell. And then up to you to agree that it is the right price at the right time, although as a small shareholder you will have little or no say. Assuming you've been an invested investor from the start, doing your homework and building trust and transparency among the Board and senior management team, you should feel confident in accepting your Board's recommendation.

The whole process can take three to six months – pretty much the same amount of time you put into due diligence and discussions before you made your first investment.

6   It is much better to be bought than to be sold.

What can go wrong on the road to exit?

There are plenty of points at which an exit can be stopped in its tracks. The most obvious is if due diligence throws up a nasty surprise, which might be down to the technology, or to legal or commercial factors. Poor governance and ill-discipline around records can kill a deal. As exit timing is unpredictable, a company should always maintain good governance and exemplary corporate, financial and commercial records.

Another problem that could put the acquirers off is if the team won't stay on. The team is the company, and in the case of the technology sector, they may be a group of very specialised individuals. This makes them mobile and desirable to other employers, so it is crucial that senior management can carry the rest of the team with them. Founders and management have to sell the acquisition as the best next step for the company, and sell the acquiring company to the team.

If the acquisition fails to go through because the team is not happy about it, this will have knock-on effects afterwards. Once they know the company is for sale, employees will be on the look out for the next threat, and might leave if they feel they will be more secure with a different employer.

An exit isn't done until the ink is dry on all the signatures and the money's safely in your bank.

> ❯ If you've had a successful exit, you can heave a sigh of relief, and then turn straight back to the other companies in your portfolio that need attention – given the statistics, some of them may be about to fail.

INVESTED INVESTOR TAKEAWAY

- The exit should be considered from the beginning.
- The best exits for the invested investor are most likely to be through acquisition.
- Valuations are complex and based on various metrics, some of which are more concrete than others.
- Investors who are not on the Board may not be heavily involved in the exit process.
- Professional advisors are important, particularly for larger deals.

AN ENTREPRENEUR'S STORY: Active Hotels exits to create Booking.com

By 2004, Active Hotels was one of the largest online hotel booking companies in Europe and growing fast – 200% per annum – and was beginning to have strategic discussions with a large number of players. Options being explored included a straight sale to a larger player, a merger with a synergistic company to help accelerate growth even further, or a potential fund raise. One of the competitors in Europe that they most respected was a Dutch company called Bookings BV, but informal discussions regarding a merger had not developed further

Meanwhile, several larger companies were circling, and Active Hotels was concerned about whether it had the resources to compete against much better funded US competitors. The safest option would be an exit, and sure enough, the first approach was made.

Active Hotels was in a good position because more than one company was interested in them, so they appointed an investment bank to organise the process and hold a beauty parade of the suitors.

Valuation metrics were complicated but a bidding war ensued, and Active Hotels eventually chose to go with US company Priceline.com (now Booking Holdings), because they felt this was the best fit.

With a large organisation behind them, what was now part of Priceline carried on expanding, and soon Andy Phillipps, co-founder of Active Hotels with Adrian Critchlow, and now CEO of Priceline's international business outside the US, was in a position to work with Priceline's management to buy the Dutch company he once considered merging with, Booking BV. The two companies were merged into what is now Booking.com, which has become one of the largest online travel companies in the world.

CHAPTER 11

Calling it quits

Have I mentioned that angel investing is a very risky business
and you're not guaranteed to make a fortune? At least a third
of your portfolio will fail, so it's time to look at different types of
failure, some of the reasons why companies fail, and what warning
signs you should look out for.

Different types of failure

When a UK company closes, it has to place an announcement in
The London Gazette, which is published daily and is the UK government's most important journal of record. This is akin to a funeral
announcement, and seeing the notices gives you a stark idea of how
common it is for companies to fail. On one day in March 2018,
there were over 200 such notices, representing the dashed hopes

and dreams of many times that number of people – founders, employees, investors, families – another reason for you to think carefully when investing in the risky world of start-ups.

> NOTICE IS HEREBY GIVEN that the Director of the Company is convening a virtual meeting of creditors to be held on 16 March 2018 at 11.00 am, for the purpose of deciding on the nomination of a liquidator.

The London Gazette accepts notices for a variety of routes to the end, including winding-up orders, appointment of administrators, receivership, creditors' voluntary liquidation and liquidation by the court. I tend to distinguish four different types of failure when an investment goes wrong – insolvent, solvent, zombie and lifestyle. They have different implications, but all of them mean I will get little or no return on my investment.

Insolvent failure

This is the worst kind of failure and can happen in several ways, all of which are costly and unpleasant. Under the UK Insolvency Act 1986, a company is insolvent if the value of its liabilities is greater than its assets (including stock and sales), although it can also be triggered by a creditor owed more than a certain amount serving notice for payment and not being paid in time.

There are instances where a company is technically insolvent but still has options to resolve the situation so there's no need to pull the plug – although professional advice should be taken to make sure this is an acceptable route to take. Trading out of insolvency can include negotiating with creditors to extend payment terms, asking debtors (i.e. customers) to pay earlier, and injecting some cash to keep things going. For very early stage companies, the latter often comes from maxing out credit cards, a familiar trait of entrepreneurs.

There are also situations where a company might be temporarily insolvent, particularly if cash gets tight before a new funding round is closed, and again every effort should be made to find a way to keep going until the new funding comes in.

Ultimately, there are penalties for directors who knowingly allow a company to continue trading if it is insolvent, but those individuals have to be behaving in demonstrably illegal ways for these sanctions to kick in – for instance, transferring money to undeclared bank accounts or moving contracts out of the insolvent company into new companies set up for the purpose.

If there appears to be no way to overcome the cash-flow problems, the company may go into liquidation, or wind up, owing money to creditors, HMRC, staff (in the form of redundancy payments) and others. This needs handling by an insolvency practitioner, who will sell the company's assets and negotiate with the creditors to pay them off as far as possible with the proceeds from selling up.

There are two ways in which an insolvent company can buy time, in the hopes that it will turn the corner and come good in the end. The first of these is to go into administration, where the administrator takes over running the business. They will usually continue to employ the same managers and will try to find the optimum solution to the crisis. This might be selling the company (probably at a knock-down price and giving little or no returns to investors), closing it if things seem hopeless, or returning it to the management and shareholders if it comes out of the doldrums.

The other way to buy time is to enter a company voluntary arrangement, or CVA. This also requires the appointment of an insolvency practitioner and involves negotiating with all the creditors to persuade them to accept reduced monthly payments and to write off any remaining debts after a certain period of time.

A less common and somewhat controversial tactic is what's known as a pre-pack administration. Here, an agreement to sell the company is made before the administrator is appointed, and the administrator sells the business to the arranged buyer or buyers once they are in position. Typically, the buyers are the company's current directors, and investors and creditors have no say in the deal. It may be the only way to save the company but it comes at a cost.

Since you're likely to be in this situation sooner or later as an investor, *The London Gazette* has a useful guide to corporate insolvency, outlining the different types and their mechanisms in more detail.

Solvent failure

A solvent failure occurs when a company has no creditors and some money in the bank but can't carry on trading for various reasons. These might include failing to monetise the product or being unable to find a market fit, but most solvent failures are caused by the investors giving up.

If a company is not getting enough money from customers to cover its operating costs and make a profit, then it has to source cash from debt, grants and equity. If equity is the only thing propping the company up, the investors may see no route to an exit and decide to call it a day. I also know of examples where it was the founders who threw in the towel – they decided not to ask the investors for more money simply for the sake of keeping going down a road they felt was leading nowhere.

There are also cases where a company is reliant on one large customer for the majority of its sales and that relationship goes wrong, or it has a large bad debt that it cannot pursue.

A solvent failure has to be wound down, something that the directors can do themselves under some circumstances, although they need to be confident that they understand fully the legal and fiduciary requirements. There are tax implications if the final amount to be distributed to shareholders after winding down is more than £25,000, including potential loss of tax relief. The Board can find ways to reduce assets to below the threshold; however, this needs to performed prudently and there is some risk for the Board. Ideally, the assets should be zero when the company closes.

If a company is solvent when it closes, you might assume that the investors would get some money out. But shareholders come last after all the creditors have been paid off, and by then there may be so little cash left that it isn't worth trying to hand any back to the investors. If, for instance, the total funding raised was £2 million, and there is £2,000 left at close, that's one thousandth of what was raised and so the shares are now worth one thousandth of what they were worth originally, that is, an initial investment of £5,000 would now be worth £5. It's expensive to distribute the remaining cash among shareholders, and an invested investor would not expect such tiny amounts to be returned. A more sensible solution might be to give what's left to charity.

The zombie

In 2016, the Association of Business Recovery Professionals (known as R3, 'Rescue, Recovery, Renewal') claimed that there were some 139,000 businesses in the UK paying only the interest on their debts, a typical sign of a zombie business. When a company is earning just enough to pay debt interest and keep creditors at bay, but not enough to pay back the capital, it won't have any spare cash to invest in growing the business.

In a zombie failure, the company keeps ticking over and covers its costs – it isn't going bust but in reality, it isn't going anywhere. The angels can't exit – their cash is trapped. In the worst cases, the founders may have taken other jobs and stopped talking to the shareholders altogether.

The company has to be closed and not allowed to stagger on because otherwise the angels cannot write off their investment against tax and offset their losses, and the closure must follow the official procedures. This can be extremely tricky if the founders have stopped talking to the shareholders. And sometimes, founders don't want to let go, even if they have lost interest in the business.

The lifestyle business

An invested investor will do all that he or she can to stop a company from becoming a lifestyle business. But it happens all too easily – the company gets to a certain sustainable size, the founders are getting paid well and they have no urge to grow the company or seek an exit. They're working regular hours and providing employment, and things are going well. There are around 5.4 million businesses in the UK that could be termed lifestyle businesses, and they are an important part of the economy. But they're not the businesses that are going to become world-beaters and create great amounts of wealth – wealth that could in turn be used to start more companies.

This is where having an angel as a director of the company is essential, as they are in a position to try and do something before the company gets too set in its ways. They may not be able to make much headway, but they might be able to force a closure if that's the only way the angels are going to get their money back.

At an angel conference in the US, there was a panel discussion on what to do about the lifestyle trap. One contributor suggested the investors take control of the company's remuneration committee and reduce the founders' salaries to $1 a year. While that would certainly give them an incentive to put some more effort into their company, the relationship between the investors and founders would be ruined for ever, and there would be no chance of the two sides joining together in any future ventures. The only option here is a sale, or a failure if the founders take it very badly.

Conversely, some angels don't want the bother of trying to push for strong scaling and an exit. They would rather take dividends from the companies they've invested in and this type of business could provide those dividends. I won't say categorically that taking dividends is wrong, but it certainly isn't the attitude I'd expect from an invested investor. Taking an income in the form of dividends is not tax efficient in the UK, as you would have to pay income tax on the dividends without recourse to any discounts offered under schemes such as EIS. In addition, this strategy means the investor may never get an exit. Without a return, they won't have the cash to recycle back into more start-ups – and I think the point of being an angel investor is to grow the quantity and quality of start-ups.

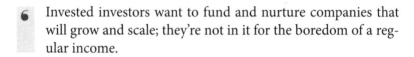

> Invested investors want to fund and nurture companies that will grow and scale; they're not in it for the boredom of a regular income.

Closing down is hard to do

You can already see from the above that the process for closing a company is long and complicated. Among the many things that have to be resolved are those relating to statutory reporting, employees, debtors, shareholders, suppliers and creditors, potential buyers and premises. Some of the tasks will be obvious, some not so obvious, and it's crucial that you take advice from someone knowledgeable, especially if a professional insolvency practitioner is not legally required.

Statutory reporting includes placing the required notices in *The London Gazette* to uncover any potential creditors, deregistering for VAT, closing the bank account and providing final accounts to HMRC. Employees must be kept informed about redundancy dates and their statutory rights, and final payroll and P45 arrangements made. Creditors will have to be contacted and the timescale and amounts for their last payments agreed. When they are informed that the company is winding down, shareholders should also be asked if they know of any potential buyers. Shareholders will also want confirmation of EIS status so that they can claim any tax relief they are due. Suppliers will have to have contracts terminated and

final payment arrangements made. Leases will have to be cancelled, hired furniture and vehicles returned, equipment sold and utility contracts closed. The list goes on – and finally, the last person to leave the building should remember to turn out the lights.

Why companies fail

Most companies fail because shareholders stop investing. CB Insights researched 101 failures, and found that more than 70% were in some way due to there being insufficient equity for the company to find a sufficient product-market fit that would allow either an exit or reliable profits. The lack of funds could be down to various reasons, including lack of market fit, meaning insufficient sales, or pricing and cost issues, but in the end investors won't continue funding companies that can't get out of these situations. This is why entrepreneurs have to keep their investors on-side or find more to keep their company going until it can stand on its own two feet – and hence why angels need reserves of more than their original investment to follow on.

Let's have a closer look at some of the reasons companies can't gain sufficient traction to keep the funds rolling in, from whatever source.

Timing Sometimes it's just too early, and the market doesn't understand the proposition. I've seen several companies where, with the best will in the world, the founders haven't been able to find a way to monetise their ideas. Even with pivots, they haven't found the sweet spot that allowed them to start making money.

In this situation, the company hasn't reached breakeven, it may not even have any revenue, and so is totally reliant on its investors. People talk about 'patient capital', investors who can afford to wait to see their return, but sometimes the waiting is simply too long and there is no exit in sight.

The technology doesn't deliver The Apple Newton (a tablet, introduced in 1993) was a good idea, but the technology of the time couldn't produce the right user experience and it didn't take off. If you compare images of the Apple Newton with the iPad, you might say that the Newton was ahead of its time and that its problem was a timing issue, but the technology couldn't deliver what was promised. Customers will only wait so long for something to work, and then they will go elsewhere.

The product/market fit is wrong The founders might not understand the market they're in sufficiently well, and so be unable to identify the right customer segments.

The market might become very crowded in an area that is taking off, and then you're likely to see a consolidation, with the survival of the fittest the order of the day. Start-ups may well get lost in all the noise, especially as they won't have the resources of companies in the same sector that have been around for longer.

> **6** 'Time and again it's the case that the management and investors have not worked hard enough at listening to the market, researching the market, and finding out exactly what customers really want. You need to understand supply chains, you need to understand the decision-making processes, you need to understand customers' budgets, and it's in the nitty-gritty where product-market fit actually goes wrong.'
>
> Rajat Malhotra, 2013 Angel Investor of the Year
> and managing partner, Wren Capital

The management team can't deliver This can happen for a number of reasons. A great idea, a fantastic vision, needs great people to execute it. If the management team is unable to hire the right people to grow the company, things could grind to a halt, or head off in the wrong direction.

Equally, the management team has to carry their employees with them and ensure everyone buys into the vision. If they can't inspire the team, they can't inspire the customers either, and a lack of enthusiastic customers singing the product's praises is a marketing headache.

When you have a situation where the founders aren't delivering, the company won't be able to raise any more funding. If potential new investors spot that the management team isn't working well, they will place their money elsewhere. The well-worn saying that investors back people more than ideas is not only relevant for the first round of investing – it is equally true at later stages in the life of a company.

You might think that an obvious answer would be to change the leadership team or bring in new skills. This is difficult and expensive. Founders are hard to get rid of; they will not only be shareholders, but also be invested emotionally and feel unable to let go of their 'baby'. People with the skills the company needs will see that it is in trouble and decide it isn't worth their while.

The balance of skills among the founders is wrong The core team simply must have a good balance of skills. In my view, two founders, one with the technical skills and one with the commercial nous, are ideal.

If the founders don't have complementary skills, there's a greater chance they'll fall out. Where both are technical or both have a commercial background, they may well end up competing, thinking they know better than the other, which is not a good recipe for progress, especially in the fast-moving and highly stressful start-up environment. They're also less likely to be able to execute the strategy, as they won't have the necessary range of skills between them.

If they bring completely different skillsets to the table, they can accept that the other knows what they're talking about, and hopefully trust each other to deliver their side of the bargain.

The founders realise they've got it wrong A better ending if you can't get a good exit is when the founders recognise that they've reached an impasse and can't find a way forward, so decide to call it a day before any more time and effort (and money) is wasted.

Sometimes, the founders realise that their business model simply won't work and choose to stop. An experienced investor might want to make sure they've explored all possible pivots, and the founders themselves may well have done so before reaching their conclusion. Even if a pivot is identified, it will almost inevitably require more funding, which could be hard to come by.

Sometimes, however, even though there may be a potential pivot, the founders can't get on board with the new vision for their company and at this point the only option is to wind things up. If the founders' aspirations aren't aligned with the new direction, forcing the pivot is really only delaying the inevitable.

The silver lining?

Some claim that if a company is going to fail, then it's better it fails early. The word 'good' may seem inappropriate, as the founders and employees will have gone through tough, and probably emotional, times and are suddenly unemployed, potentially causing financial problems. However, as the cliché goes, life is not a rehearsal. Or, to put it another way, we all should be concerned about the opportunity cost of time.

What the founders will have learned from a failure is actually valuable, although they won't think so at the time. They will inevitably have made mistakes and will have gained useful knowledge as a result. For instance, if the failure was down to the loss, or failure itself, of a big customer, that might suggest that the founders had little control over what happened, but this is not necessarily the case. The founders should come away understanding the need to avoid being too reliant on any one customer and the dangers of advancing too much trade credit.

> **TRANSPARENCY TAKEAWAY**
>
> Founders should be honest and transparent about what they have learned from earlier mistakes. If they claim that a previous failure was nothing to do with them, they are either failing my transparency test or deluded.

> ❛ 'Sometimes it takes a failure to understand a success.'
> Simon Murdoch, Episode 1 Ventures

There's another interesting angle to failures – what they can tell you about successes. Entrepreneurs who have been successful first time round might be surprised when their second venture fails, but they can look back on the earlier success to identify where they made the right decisions and where they got lucky, and compare that with what they've done this time. Then they should be well equipped for their next start-up, or have plenty of useful experience to pass on to their investees if they go down the invested investor route.

> 6 An elegant failure is one where the company is solvent when it closes, and the founders remain investible because they are transparent and honest about what they've learned. Such a failure may also leave a legacy in the form of a problem being solved even though the company is no longer part of the solution.

> Successes and failures are inescapable in the world of the invested investor, but neither should mean the end of the journey. Invested investors will want to, and indeed should, go round again.

Time for the final chapter – which is really only the beginning.

INVESTED INVESTOR TAKEAWAY

- Many companies fail, and most of the companies in your portfolio will not make it to a successful exit.
- Failures can be insolvent or solvent. An investment can also be considered a failure if the company earns just enough to keep ticking over (the zombie), or if it becomes a lifestyle business and maintains the status quo through minimal growth.
- There are statutory procedures to follow when closing a business.

AN ENTREPRENEUR'S STORY:
The elegant failure

Ready Steady Mums was set up by entrepreneur and business coach Katy Tuncer in 2011. Its eventual demise was handled very carefully – so carefully, in fact, that several of her investors (who had lost all their money) said they'd be willing to back her next time around. And Ready Steady Mums still delivers on her vision, just in a different way. How did she manage such an elegant failure?

Katy's background includes the army, the Metropolitan Police and McKinsey, and along the way, she learned that she loves starting new things. She had the idea for Ready Steady Mums when she was pregnant with the first of her four sons. She couldn't find the support she wanted to help her keep fit during and after pregnancy, and realised she'd found a gap in the market that needed filling. Her idea was for a virtual personal trainer, with a tailored programme for pregnant women and mothers that would boost their fitness and well-being as their bodies went through major changes. She began to design the system while she was pregnant, and enlisted the help of a friend from university to do the programming and develop a prototype.

Her ideas were further refined after she had given birth, when she noted the importance of community support for new mothers. She began to run a local group to test her ideas, and when one of her participants moved, they set up a second group at their new location. Another participant set up another group that grew quickly, so now there was a model for rolling the programme out.

It wasn't long before there were some 20 groups, and Katy thought it was time to try turning her ideas for a virtual personal trainer into a business. Yet somehow she couldn't get traction. Mothers were happily joining the groups, but they weren't paying for the online trainer side of the offering. Katy tried a subscription model, pay as you go, and even had a deal with Mothercare, but participants still didn't want to pay for the trainer.

Katy wanted to launch a proper marketing campaign, rather than relying on word of mouth as she had up to now. And she wanted to improve the user experience (UX) for her virtual trainer programme. The programme had been developed in conjunction with gynaecologists and fitness experts, and the content was excellent, so surely there should be a way to make it a saleable proposition?

In the meantime, she was still working a full-time job and had her second son, so she was looking for a way to grow the team to take Ready Steady Mums to the next level. To do this, she needed to raise some funds. She had had several conversations with business angels, none of which had produced any investment, but one of the angels pointed out that she already had some of the ingredients for a successful crowdfunding campaign, including endorsements from the communities she had set up.

This was 2013, early days for crowdfunding, and there were only a few active platforms at the time. Katy found them to be very sales-driven, but singled out Seedrs and CrowdCube. Eventually, she picked Seedrs, as they had a nominee structure and would do the legal work and distribute shares to investors. She put a lot of effort into developing a video pitch and pulled together a stellar group of advisors who were all willing to appear on the video endorsing Katy and her business. And Katy herself did everything she could to spread the word – including going up to strangers in the street to tell them about her business.

The Seedrs crowdfunding campaign raised £57,000, £7,000 over Katy's target. There were a lot of £10 investors, and although they weren't putting much money in, Katy assumed – hoped – they would tell their friends and colleagues and spread the word. Around ten investors put in £1,000 or more, but before they did so, they wanted to talk to her about the business – frequently a 'grilling', as Katy put it.

The fundraising took about three months, and then Seedrs took six weeks to pass on the money, resulting in a cash flow problem for Katy that she bridged with a director's loan – and then found she couldn't pay herself back out of the money raised as that was specifically excluded from the deal. Nevertheless, Katy had exceeded her fundraising target and was ready to get going in early summer 2013.

So what went wrong?

The first thing Katy needed to do was grow the team, and things started well, with three employees and the marketing and UX development under way. But Katy soon recognised that her expectations of creating a team of like-minded people who owned the vision, like she did, and had the same obsessive dedication to making it work were unrealistic.

And then the problems really started. With a very small team, if relationships sour, they have a massive impact on the whole project, and this was what happened. Disagreements and arguments escalated, and it was impossible to reach agreement on a number of issues, not least how best to do things. Katy says she fell into the trap of trying to keep everyone happy and not being tough enough. It wasn't long before she was feeling exhausted, trying to pretend it was all fine while picking up all the dropped balls and working harder and harder herself.

Although Katy had a board of exceptionally good advisors, they were all voluntary and none had been made a director of the company. This too, in retrospect, was a mistake. A director with more experience might have been able to nip the personnel problems in the bud, and help Katy take the difficult step of letting someone go for the good of the business.

A last learning point for Katy was the need to identify clearly where efforts should be focused to give the best chances of succeeding. This is where I came in – we met at a dinner where Katy was talking about her crowdfunding experience. She got in touch after the dinner and we started to chat – I wanted her coaching expertise to help me prioritise my time and say 'no' more often, and she was keen to get some insights into what she might do to get Ready Steady Mums back on track. It should be said that Katy never asked me for investment. Which was just as well, as I would have said 'no' (perhaps she realised that already?). She didn't fit my criteria, since Ready

Steady Mums was B2C, not deep tech, and had a single (and part-time) founder.

Our discussions revealed that Katy was constantly improving non-critical elements and functions, but this did not help the bottom line. I worked with her to identify what she had to achieve in order for the business to survive – and face the cruel realisation that if those KPIs weren't achieved, then it would be time to shut the business.

Like many new entrepreneurs, Katy was surprised at how quickly the money ran out, and also at how quickly conflict could escalate into serious problems for the business. But she says she'll never know if the failure was down to difficulties within the team, or because they hadn't found the right product/market fit.

Closing the business was deeply painful and Katy hated doing it, but she appreciated having clear decision lines that confirmed the decision to close was the right one.

I'm an advocate for transparency and openness, so I recommended she telephone her larger investors – those who had given her a grilling previously – and tell them what had happened. She found the prospect terrifying, and spent some time preparing what she would say before she picked up the phone and made the first call.

To her great surprise, the first investor she called didn't explode with anger. They thanked her for calling, said they'd never have expected a founder to ring with the bad news – they'd be more likely to hide and never get in contact again. In fact, the investor said they were so impressed with Katy's explanation of what had gone wrong and what she'd learned that they offered to back her again if she started a new venture.

Almost all Katy's investors had similar reactions, although she was still very nervous before she made each call. Responses included noting that Katy had done everything to try and make the business work, that they hadn't gone in with their eyes shut, and thanking her for telling them what had happened. They were sophisticated investors who knew that start-ups were risky things. And almost all said, 'Call me next time'.

So Katy closed her company with very mixed feelings. The end was just solvent, so she didn't close owing any money, but there was a personal cost because she was still disappointed that her idea hadn't come to fruition. She has kept in touch with her investors, and continues to operate and think like an entrepreneur. She now thinks about failure in a much more healthy way, and uses her journey to inform her coaching practice and inspire others.

And Ready Steady Mums is still going, albeit in a different form from the one that Katy envisaged. The Institute of Health Visiting, a charity, had worked with Katy as she built her communities of mothers, and continued the groups after Katy had closed the business. There are now more than 100 volunteer-led Ready Steady Mums groups in the UK, and Katy's vision of delivering mental and physical health benefits to pregnant women and young mothers continues to develop a life of its own.

CHAPTER 12

The merry-go-round

The key messages I want you to have picked up having read this far are that angel investing is difficult, time-consuming and stressful, and requires transparency and openness on all sides. But I hope you've also picked up that it's a fantastic opportunity to learn a new set of skills, put your own experience to good use, and grow amazing businesses that support the local and wider economy.

The crucial word there is the plural, businesses – at the risk of repeating myself, putting all your eggs in one basket is almost guaranteed to fail. By now, you should understand this. You should also understand that you can't wait for your first investment to exit before you make your next one. You have to build a portfolio

of investments to have a chance of success, and that means going round again, and soon.

The portfolio imperative

We've talked about the numbers before, and the statistics behind recommending you build a portfolio of investments of at least 15 companies, and preferably 20 or more.

If you're a new investor, that can seem rather daunting. It might take you a year or more to find and close your first investment, and if each one takes a year, you might feel you'll be too old for the fray by the time you've found 15, let alone 20. Building a portfolio can also seem daunting because you know that if it takes a few years before you see whether that first investment is going to make it past the failure zone, and then a few more years before you see the glimmerings of an exit, then how are you going to learn all the lessons you need to learn about investing before you take the plunge again?

There are no easy answers – you haven't got time to wait and see what happens in your first investment before you add another, and another, to your portfolio. There's no convenient feedback loop diagram that goes 'invest – learn – exit – invest again'; it's much messier than that. However, there are ways to make it easier, even though you'll still have to put in the time and effort.

Your first proper angel investment will take a while and you need to accept that and not rush. Crowdfunding investments are much quicker to source, but will be no quicker to succeed and, although the evidence will take a few more years to appear, my feeling is that the success ratio for some crowdfunding platforms will be lower. I put them in a different category, as they are rarely as hands-on as an invested investor should be.

To get started as an invested investor, you will have looked around in your neighbourhood and in your sector for other angels to talk to and invest with. You will have started going to the types of events where entrepreneurs and investors mingle, and you will have begun building a network of interested and interesting people across the spectrum from entrepreneur to investor.

All that effort will serve as the foundation for your subsequent investments. Your networks will continue to build, you'll be learning from others' war stories, and you'll be asking different questions to add to what you already know. You'll still be on the hunt for excellent teams and ideas with commercial potential, but you'll already have a better perspective on what you're looking for.

Having made one investment also marks you out in the ecosystem, so founders might start looking for you. Well-known investors and VC funds get hundreds and even thousands of approaches each year; some angels manage their privacy so well they get barely any, but rely on their carefully built network to source deals. You will know how comfortable you feel about going public with your investments and how you want to position yourself.

These days, more angels are putting up websites like mine, where they list their portfolio and their investment criteria. If you decide to go down this route be aware that, despite specifying your criteria, it will generate irrelevant contacts and you will have to be ruthless in rejecting those. However, the more business plans you see, the more you learn how to separate the good from the fanciful. And the more founders you interact with, the more chances you've got to find someone and something really good to invest in.

As you build your portfolio, the question of how much time to devote to each company will become increasingly important. You will start to get a better idea of how much time your current investments take up, and how much time you have left to spend searching for new companies to add to your list. Investors who have a large portfolio and run the whole thing on their own are rare.

I'd say the average amount of time spent working with a company if you're on the Board is one half to two days per month, depending on the stage of the company and what is happening. So if you have 15 companies in your portfolio, you could find pretty much the whole month taken up with reviewing papers and attending meetings. That doesn't leave much spare time for due diligence on any new prospects, so you'll quickly find that balancing your commitments is essential – hence the importance of co-investing alongside others who can help spread the load. If you've made your first investment on your own, put more effort into finding like-minded angels in your region and preferred sector so you can co-invest in future and build a larger portfolio. At the time of writing, I am on five start-up Boards as a director and two as an observer.

How to make the most of what you learn

Learn all the time, from other investors, from the entrepreneurs you admire, from the entrepreneurs you invest in, and from just about anyone else involved in start-ups and growing businesses. You can also learn from yourself, by looking at your own data.

You should develop the habit of keeping good records of your investments. Once you've got a few companies in your portfolio, you start to build a collection of information that can provide useful insights when you're thinking about following on, or making a new investment. I have a one-page spreadsheet that summarises the basics on all my portfolio companies so that I can see the overall status of my investments at a glance. I also include relevant information about the founders, other shareholders and results.

A basic overview spreadsheet

- Name of company
- Date formed
- Date closed/sold
- Overview of company and sector
- My shareholding as a percentage of the company
- Success as multiple, if exited
- Some financial metrics – revenue, losses, etc.
- Founding team
- Investor director
- My relevant skills
- Their skills

What have I learned from my spreadsheet? I can see how often I've invested outside my sector and whether or not that has been successful. I can interrogate my own biases – how many of my founders are STEM graduates? How many are graduates at all? How many have MBAs? (Answer to that last question, very few.) How many are women? I can also review the different criteria against whether the companies had a successful exit or not, and that helps when I look at new companies. The patterns in your own investing only reveal themselves when you look at the big picture in this way, and they can surprise you.

It's not just portfolio companies, though. I also keep records of deals that went as far as due diligence, even if I didn't end up investing, to help understand where they fell down. In an ideal world – if there were more than 24 hours in the day, perhaps – I'd follow all those companies as well to note what happened to them. While

I do tend to notice when a company I turned down has a good exit (and think, 'Well done' rather than, 'Damn, missed that one'), I could learn more if I also kept track of the others, noting the failures and the also-rans. If I turned them down and they succeeded, what did I miss? Was it due to a pivot that I couldn't have foreseen at the time? If they failed, did they fail for the reasons I suspected, the reasons that put me off investing? Or did they fail because of something completely different, something that I should watch out for in future?

I also file all the emails I get with business plans. Even if I don't follow them up, they are there as background data if I'm approached by the same company, or the same founders with a different idea, in the future. This can form part of my own due diligence to supplement what's available in the public domain.

If you've been an entrepreneur, you can also learn from your own track record before starting to invest in other new businesses. As I mentioned before, I kept a detailed diary of what happened in my first company, Camdata, and every now and then I look at it to remind myself of what can go wrong and why.

There's no point in learning unless you remember to apply those lessons when a new situation comes up. But even an experienced invested investor makes mistakes. It's all too easy to get lulled into a false sense of security, confident that things are under control. That's a very dangerous position to be in – thinking you know what you're doing and haven't anything more to learn is the worst thing for an invested investor. And it can be really painful – and expensive – when things do go pear-shaped.

One very experienced – and frequently successful – investor I know shared his lessons when a business he'd invested in went into administration. First, choose your founders carefully. Do they listen? Are they overconfident? Are they arrogant? Do they trust too easily? Are they thinking critically about potential investors and what they might bring with them? Can they sell? Second, read

the small print on the key person insurance – will it pay out if you need it? Third, if the company needs a bail out, make sure the terms are sensible – don't be too generous. Finally, if management keeps making the same mistakes – change the management.

The merry-go-round

Back in Chapter 1, I told you the story of my company Camdata and its rollercoaster ride through recession, cash flow crises, liquidation and finally emerging as a business that washes its face but isn't going to change the world. Since 1980, I've been involved in over 75 businesses as entrepreneur or investor, some of which I firmly believe are going to change the world, and I hope that I've played a part, however small, in that success.

I've seen a pattern among my fellow invested investors that mirrors mine. Many of us have been at the coalface as entrepreneurs, although some have been equally successful coming from a corporate background. We like growing businesses and the challenges that brings, but we also like leveraging our experience so that more start-ups can benefit. And we like to give back.

> ❛ 'My angel investors and my Board have given me massive amounts of advice and support, when you could argue that it was irrational to do so. I did feel, and I still do, that once you've "made it" there's a responsibility to give something back to the ecosystem.'
>
> Andy Phillipps, entrepreneur and investor

I'm frequently asked to speak at events around the world in places that are seeking to develop a more entrepreneurial ecosystem, because investment is the key to starting and growing more companies. Regions that want to support their innovators understand that they need more smart capital, the sort that invested investors bring. They also actively seek to learn from other, more entrepreneurial regions, just as you should actively seek to learn from experienced investors as you begin your investing journey.

There are other ways to give back. Richard Lucas, a serial investor based in Poland since 1991, has worked to promote entrepreneurship in his adopted homeland and elsewhere as a volunteer. He supports many projects in schools and universities to encourage enterprise. He served on the honorary committee for Global Entrepreneurship Week Poland, the advisory board of Startup Poland, is an ambassador for the Krakow Startup Community Foundation, and set up CAMentrepreneurs to encourage entrepreneurship among university alumni worldwide.

If, like many angels, you've started investing after a successful career doing something else, you will need to think about the future. When do you stop? There will always be good ideas out there, and there will always be enthusiastic entrepreneurs looking to start businesses and change the world.

Once you've built up your portfolio, and realised how much of your time it takes up, then you should think carefully about how many times you go back to 'Go' and start again. At some point, you will come to realise that it might be time to wind down.

Perhaps it's not so much a rollercoaster as a merry-go-round – we keep going round and round again, the horses going up and down in time to the music, with those of us on the ride hoping to get off at the right moment.

As for me, I plan to stop first-round investing when I reach 65, and then spend the next ten years or so running down my portfolio as the companies in it exit. I doubt I'll stop completely – even when I get to the point where I have no investments. I imagine I'll still be going to events and chatting to entrepreneurs and investors about the challenges they're facing whenever I get the opportunity – my experience won't become redundant just because I no longer have active investments. But by the time I'm 75, I hope to be spending more time with my family, more time skiing, diving and hiking, and a lot less time wading through business plans.

The Invested Investor rules of angel investing

Be transparent. I'm convinced that transparency and openness lie at the heart of the vast majority of successful investor-investee relationships, so make this your core value.

Be fair. With entrepreneurs, fellow angels and with customers. Bad behaviour will come back and bite you in the years of investing and cooperation ahead.

Learn. Explore different ways to learn about investing – through crowdfunding, investor forums, angel groups and, hopefully, an angel mentor who will provide guidance and advice.

Work hard. Due diligence, as the name suggests, requires you to be diligent. Being an invested investor is a lot more time-consuming than most people imagine.

Trust your instincts – up to a point. Listen to your gut feelings about an entrepreneur as well as studying the data. Use both in your decision – don't just rely on one or the other.

Start! There's only so much you can learn from other people and the internet, then you have to start learning from your own experience. If you don't write that first cheque, what's the point?

Invest only what you can afford to lose. Your investment pot must include enough for second and possibly third rounds in every investment.

Consider each investment lost once it is made. Although an angel with a large and diverse portfolio may achieve over 20% annual return on capital, assuming that investments are lost means that every positive exit is a pleasant surprise.

Invest with other angels. Co-investing not only makes more cash available in the early rounds, it also brings more diverse experiences and skills to support the company.

Be ready to fail. All experienced investors know that some, possibly many, of their companies will fail.

Don't blame others when things go wrong. Each investor makes their own decision to invest – if you end up blaming someone, stop investing.

Be ready to succeed. If you're lucky, you will have one or more stars in your portfolio, and those successes will give you more funds to invest.

Keep going. If at first… and all that.

Glossary

A round See **Funding round**.

Angel investor An individual who invests their own money in start-up companies or entrepreneurs. The term 'angel' was originally used to refer to investors who funded theatrical productions.

Bad leaver See **Good leaver/bad leaver**.

Board observer Member of the Board without voting rights, but who plays an active part in guiding and advising the company during Board meetings.

Breakeven When a company reaches the point where it funds itself through sales. Companies can be funded via four sources – equity (i.e. investment), debt, grants or customers. Equity will run out if the investors lose faith (around three-quarters of all company failures are due to investors stopping funding), debt has to be paid back, grants are finite and only applicable in some situations, so a company has to find customers, or breakeven, to survive.

Burn rate The rate at which a company spends investment capital on operating costs (staff, premises, cost of sale of goods, etc.) less any sales income. This varies from month to month but gives an indication of the Runway.

Cap table Capitalisation table – a spreadsheet showing ownership of a company, including all share types plus the maximum number of options that may be awarded. This also includes how much was paid for the shares and will be updated at each round.

Deferred share A share that is only paid back during bankruptcy proceedings if there is any residue after holders of common and preference shares have been paid.

Dilution When current shareholders will own a smaller percentage of the company after new shares have been issued and sold. This will also happen when options are exercised.

Down round A funding round where the valuation of the company is lower than it was in the preceding round.

Drag-along right A right that enables majority shareholders to force minority shareholders to sell their shares when the company is sold or exits.

Earn out A contractual provision whereby the shareholders who sell a company are entitled to future payments if certain specified milestones are met. The seller earns part of the purchase price, for instance by staying with the company for a defined period of time in order to achieve the stipulated milestones.

Exit When ownership of a company transfers to new owners, either another company, a different group of investors, or to the public via an initial public offering (IPO).

Follow on A second or subsequent investment made in a company by the same investor providing more funds.

Funding round A period of raising money to fund development of a company that ends when the money has been raised. Funding rounds are frequently given labels that indicate the stage of the company (seed, series A, series B, etc.). Not all companies go through all the stages, particularly if they reach profitability earlier than expected.

Good leaver/bad leaver A provision in the shareholders' agreement that formally defines how the shares owned by an employee, typically a founder, are redistributed when that person leaves the company. The provision is intended to incentivise the key people in a start-up to remain with the company at least until certain milestones are reached, and to deter them from leaving early or breaching their service agreements. Typically, a good leaver is one who leaves due to circumstances beyond their control; a bad leaver is one who resigns or contravenes acceptable business practices.

Initial Public Offering (IPO) The first time a company offers its shares to the public.

Intangible assets An asset that is not physical, such as intellectual property (IP), copyrights, trademarks, brand recognition.

Investor director A member of the Board who is the representative of a group of investors (commonly all).

Lifestyle business One in which the founders reach a point where they're getting a comfortable income from the business and working sensible hours, but are not motivated to grow the business or scale strongly. Around 5.4 million businesses in the UK fit this description. These businesses provide returns for their investors and support the local and national economy, but they are not the type of growth businesses that invested investors should be looking to fund.

Non-executive director A member of the Board who is not part of the executive team and therefore does not play a part in the day-to-day running of the organisation. Their role is to provide independent strategic advice, and they are normally chosen for the particular experiences and connections they can bring to the company. They may be paid for their services, but are not considered employees of the company.

Option The right to buy a share or a specified number of shares at a particular price by or on a particular date or event.

Ordinary share A share in the ownership of a company that entitles the possessor to vote and to receive dividends (if issued), and to share in the proceeds of an exit after any preference shares have been settled.

Paid up capital The amount of money a company has received in exchange for shares.

Pivot When a company changes direction because the original business model isn't working.

Pre-emption rights The right of existing shareholders to buy some or all of a new issue of shares in a company before other investors are invited to buy.

Preference shares Shares that take precedence over ordinary shares when dividends are issued, when the proceeds of an exit are distributed, or when a company is closed and remaining assets are sold off and funds released to pay back investors.

Runway The amount of time a company has until the cash runs out and either more money has to be raised or the company has to close.

Scale-up A company that is growing fast – defined by the OECD as having an annualised growth rate of 20% over the preceding three years and at least ten employees at the beginning of that period. Such high-growth firms are sometimes referred to as gazelles.

Seed funding Very early funding, typically provided by those closest to a start-up – family, friends, the start-up team themselves.

Series A, B, C, etc. Series A is usually the first significant injection of venture capital funding. It can be followed by series B, C, etc.

Shareholders' agreement A legally binding document signed by the investors and founders of a company that defines how ownership of the company is distributed between investors and founders, and reflects what has been agreed in the term sheet.

Sweat equity The non-financial contribution put into a company by the founders as a way to earn their share of the ownership of the company.

Tag-along The right for a minority shareholder to sell their shares when a major shareholder sells. The minority shareholder is not obliged to sell their shares, unlike a drag-along clause, but may do so if they wish.

Term sheet A mostly non-binding document that sets out the deal to be completed between investors and founders. The legally binding shareholders' agreement is based on the term sheet.

Underwater Stock options are said to be underwater when the price of shares in the company falls below the price of the options.

Unicorn A privately held company with a valuation of $1 billion or more.

Venture capital A pool of funds invested by professional managers (whereas angels typically invest their own money).

Vesting When options are vested over a certain amount of time, they cannot be exercised (bought) until the end of the vesting period is reached. The options may be exercised in tranches during that time, for instance one-third after two years, another third after one more year, and the rest after a total of four years, or all in a single tranche at the end of the vesting period.

Takeaways and templates

Are you ready to put on your wings?

- Being an invested investor is not easy and takes hard work.
- You have a lot to learn.
- Make sure that you understand the risks associated with early stage investing.
- Build a portfolio.
- Keep money back for each of the companies in your portfolio so that you can follow on in later funding rounds.

Funder meets founder

- Build a broad and deep network of contacts from all parts of the ecosystem.
- Develop a set of investment criteria that works for you.
- Create your own ideal pitch deck template to help assess those sent to you.
- Don't be too inflexible and miss an opportunity because it isn't a perfect fit.

My criteria for investing in technology start-ups

The team
- High growth ambitions
- Outstanding team of at least two people
- UK legal structure
- Founders based in the UK
- Deep trust and respect for the investor director (whether they are yet to be chosen or already in post)
- Understanding of the ratio between customer lifetime value (CLV) and cost of customer acquisition (CCA)

The product
- Evidence of a large market
- Defensibility
- In technology (my sector)
- B2B or (rarely) B2B2C
- Deep product technology

The finances
- Early stage income
- Pre-money valuation up to a maximum of £2 million
- Plan for a minimum 10x valuation increase over 4–10 years
- No platforms that charge fees
- Syndicated
- Very few non-disclosure agreements (NDAs)

What I like to see in a pitch deck

Slide 1   Images of market and/or product and/or team, with company name/logo, mission, vision

Slide 2   Team – photos, education, background; any non-executive directors or advisors who have already been appointed or are guaranteed to be appointed after the round closes

Slide 3   The unmet need. Could be an illustration of business/consumer journey containing 'pain' that needs healing

Slide 4   Your solution

5–10 ancillary slides covering:

- Market size – bottom up, rather than top down (selling to 0.1% of all mobile phone users is a big number, but not credible)
- Route to market
- Competition
- Pricing
- Cost of customer acquisition and customer lifetime value
- Finances 1: use of investment capital over the 12–18 months to the next round

- Finances 2: three- or five-year plan with sales, gross margin, overheads and losses/profits (Investors rarely believe this, and it will be wrong anyway, but it shows you have thought through the longer term. A simple graph will suffice)
- Defensibility
- Product (not service, although some products may have an element of service income, for instance customer adoption and/or maintenance)
- Progress to date if you are already trading
- Exit planning (again, rarely correct, but shows you intend to exit)

Final slide Overview of team, market, tech and financial (or other) 'ask'

Due diligence

- Be open with your entrepreneurs about how you will conduct due diligence, the topics to be covered and what you find as you proceed.
- Look at the team first; if it's the wrong team, don't invest.
- If the opportunity is in tech, identify if the product is ready for market or still in development.
- Investigate the defensibility of the business idea or product.
- Make sure that market expectations are realistic.
- Look for a sustainable business model.
- Be confident about the finances and plans for how the investment will be spent.
- Don't waste time regretting the ones that got away.

Due diligence basics

- The team
- The technology
- The defensibility
- The market
- The business
- The finances

What you want in a team

- Passion
- Drive
- Transparency and honesty
- Awareness of their own limitations
- Willingness to learn
- Willingness to listen
- Balanced appetite for risk
- Ability to inspire

Finance factors to look at

- Realistic gross margins, calculated correctly
- Realistic channel costs
- Price erosion/cost increases considered
- Risks in existing commercial agreements evaluated
- Presence of exclusivities
- Clean investment structure with alignment of interests
- Debt
- Recruitment budget
- IP protection and progression budget

Co-investing

- Don't invest on your own – find co-investors to share the financial and administrative load.
- Do due diligence on the entrepreneurs and the business plan, and also on your co-investors.
- Start small – three to four co-investors is right at the very beginning.
- Don't be the deal lead until you are ready, and confident that you know what to do.
- Make sure that the deal lead is the person most suited to the opportunity.
- Reach a mutually agreed valuation that is as accurate as possible under the circumstances.

The paperwork

- The three essential legal documents are the shareholders' agreement, the articles of association and the disclosure letter.
- Service agreements and key man insurance may be important.
- The term sheet is the crucial foundation document for the shareholders' agreement and articles of association.
- Don't forget to include good leaver/bad leaver provisions.

The essentials

There are three essential legal documents in an investor/investee relationship:

- Shareholders' agreement, also known as the investment agreement (IA) or subscription agreement (SA)
- Articles of association
- Disclosure letter

In addition to these, you will need service agreements and possibly key man insurance.

But the key to getting these three documents right is the term sheet.

My term sheet template

- Investment
- Conditions of investment
- Terms of investment
- Confidentiality
- Applicable law
- Expiry date
- Exclusivity
- No intention to create legal relations
- Exclusion of representations and warranties
- Signature pages
- Appendices

Putting the Board together

- The Board is there to guide and advise. It is also there to provide monitoring, governance and control.
- The Board is composed of representatives from the investors and the founders, and will include an investor director.
- Board observers do not have a vote, but are expected to contribute.
- Board packs are essential, even though they may seem time-consuming to founders of start-up companies.
- The Board, and particularly the investor director, are responsible for keeping all investors informed.
- Regular, minuted Board meetings can form essential collateral when negotiating later funding rounds or an exit.

Who's who on the Board?

- *Directors* Those in charge, including some or all of the founders and representatives from among the investors. All directors will be registered with Companies House as Board members, giving them legal responsibilities, and putting their names in the public domain. All directors are obliged to attend all Board meetings. Remember, the founders are employees – the company is managed by the Board and not vice versa.
- *Founder director(s)* Those chosen from among and by the founders of the company, commonly all the founders at the start.
- *Investor directors* One or more of the investors (but usually only one), chosen by the group of investors to represent their interests on the Board. They will have the ability to veto some actions.
- *Board observers* Representatives of the investors who provide input to the Board but don't have voting rights, and who report back to the investors. They should receive most of the Board communications, such as the Board information pack, including trading updates and status reports. Observers are not obliged to attend every Board meeting, but are not passive, as the

name suggests. Observers are expected to be fully engaged and
contribute when they do attend.

- *Chair of the Board* Often an independent director, chosen by
mutual agreement by the founder director(s) and the investor
director(s). There are arguments for and against the chair being a
shareholder. The argument for is that the chair is fully aligned with
the shareholder value growth of the company; against is the lack of
true independence that being a shareholder brings.

Sample Board agenda

1. Conflicts of interest (seems formal but may become more
   important later as the Board grows). For instance, some of my
   portfolio companies are customers of one of the companies I
   chair.
2. Accepting minutes of last meeting
3. Actions arising (unless covered elsewhere in the agenda)
4. Sales report* – brief overview of items that the Board needs to
   hear: lost orders or sales (and the reasons), contacts needed,
   partners/re-sellers, sales pipeline, foreign forays, successes
5. Marketing report*
6. Technology report*
7. Human resources (HR) report*
8. Finance report*§
9. Infrastructure* – premises, IT, insurance, health and safety
   compliance, etc.
10. Risk register* – informal early on, becoming more formal later
11. Strategy – probably to discuss output from the advisory panel,
    if there is one, although the Board needs to own and adopt the
    outcomes formally
12. Any other business
13. Date/time/place of next meeting

* Reports and information pertinent to these items should be sent
out to Board members several days ahead of the meeting. Too

often the pack arrives late the night before. This is bad practice, but founders have many priorities, and I commonly read the board pack on the train journey to the meeting.

§ The finance report should include profit and loss (year to date and last month, both against budget), balance sheet to end of previous month, creditors, debtors and cash flow forecast (quarterly). I am very keen on seeing how debtors (assuming trade credit is given) are ageing (i.e. which customers are more than a month overdue in paying), as this may show the company is invoicing too early, that customers are not happy with what the company is providing, or that the company is not chasing customers for money (too many businesses wait until they are chased for payment, even the multinational ones). Remember that customer money is much better in your bank account than theirs and no investor wants to provide equity to cover working capital – that should be provided by customers.

What I expect in a shareholders' update

Portfolio Co Ltd: Report to Investors March 20XX

1. Executive summary

    What is our 'ask'? How can the shareholders help? There doesn't have to be an ask, but most shareholders love being able to help and it makes them feel they are on the same journey.

    What are the highlights of the year to date? Reaching profitability? Milestones? R&D grants or other awards? Key personnel hires?

    What are the overall financials? How much cash is there in the bank? What is the cash runway? What are the latest revenue figures? Are there profits on sales? What is the target for the year? When is the next equity round needed? Remember that, until a company reaches breakeven, the losses need to be funded by equity (potentially plus grants).

    How is product development progressing?

    What is the bigger picture? Regulatory environment, approvals, wider economic situation?

2. Sales strategy and distribution
   How is the sales strategy reflecting the business model? Has either had to be adapted due to changing circumstances? Who is/are the key figure(s) driving sales? What shareholder input might be useful?
   How is/are distribution channels developing? Is progress slow, fast, as expected? Are there any roadblocks in the distribution channels?
   Is there progress in international distribution? If so, what has happened since the last update?
3. Marketing, PR and direct sales approaches
   What marketing activities have been undertaken? What feedback/response has been recorded? What metrics are being used to track effectiveness?
   How is PR integrated with marketing? What media coverage has been secured? Are there any new relationships developing with key journalists, media outlets or spokespeople?
   What are the website, social media and other online metrics? Where are leads coming from?
4. Product development and procurement
   How is product development going? How are industry standards being met? How are innovations outside industry standards being met by the industry and customers?
   If appropriate, has there been progress in manufacturing? Where is manufacturing taking place? How are manufacturing costs in comparison to previous expectations? What are the logistics around product delivery? What areas have been noted for improvement? There may also be quality and customer service metrics to evaluate.
5. Financials – against forecasts and budget, and may include financial KPI tracking.
   Cash in the bank
   Sales figures
   Gross margin

P&L

Balance sheet against budget

Forecast for the next quarter

Projections for revenues and how those revenues, if realised, might be used to grow the company

And most importantly, if not at breakeven, what is the runway – the time until the cash runs out and either more money has been raised or the company closes.

6. Can you help?

An extended version of the 'ask' in the executive summary. What might the investors do to help the company? What introductions could they make that would be useful at this stage? Can they help source needed skills?

Growing pains

- Building the team is a key early activity, and you can help with suggestions and by encouraging diversity.
- Proving the technology or concept can take time and possibly more money.
- Proving the market may require your help with contacts and introductions.
- Founder-CEOs rarely stay in position all the way through to exit. Do your best to help them grow with the role, but be prepared to have difficult conversations.

The pivot

- A pivot is not a sign of failure – many, if not most, businesses pivot on their way to optimising the model.
- Pivots can be driven by a number of factors, including the technology, the market and the business model.
- Founders and investors should be aware when a pivot becomes necessary.
- Pivots may require additional funding.

The successful exit

- The exit should be considered from the beginning.
- The best exits for the invested investor are most likely to be through acquisition.
- Valuations are complex and based on various metrics, some of which are more concrete than others.
- Investors who are not on the Board may not be heavily involved in the exit process.
- Professional advisors are important, particularly for larger deals.

Advisors and exits

Reasons to have advisors

- They have very good contacts and can find potential acquirers for the company – to the extent where they can make a significant difference to the size of the offer on larger deals.
- They ensure that the information package – the prospectus – for the company is fit for purpose.
- They are independent, so can negotiate objectively during an auction (which is difficult for founders to do as there is so much emotion involved).
- They release the executive team from a lot of the work involved in preparing for an exit, allowing them to maintain their focus on running the company. This can be essential for the company's future if the exit doesn't happen.

Reasons not to have advisors

- The deal isn't big enough for them – or their fees will take too big a chunk of your return.
- There is enough skill on the Board to cover what's needed.

Calling it quits

- Many companies fail, and most of the companies in your portfolio will not make it to a successful exit.

- Failures can be insolvent or solvent. An investment can also be considered a failure if the company earns just enough to keep ticking over (the zombie), or if it becomes a lifestyle business and maintains the status quo through minimal growth.
- There are statutory procedures to follow when closing a business.

The merry-go-round
Learning from your investing experiences
- Name of company
- Date formed
- Date closed/sold
- Overview of company
- My shareholding as a percentage of the company
- Success as multiple, if exited
- Some financial metrics – revenue, losses, etc.
- Founding team
- Investor director
- My relevant skills
- Their skills

The Invested Investor rules of angel investing

Be transparent. I'm convinced that transparency and openness lie at the heart of the vast majority of successful investor-investee relationships, so make this your core value.

Be fair. With entrepreneurs, fellow angels and with customers. Bad behaviour will come back and bite you in the years of investing and cooperation ahead.

Learn. Explore different ways to learn about investing – through crowdfunding, investor forums, angel groups and, hopefully, an angel mentor who will provide guidance and advice.

Work hard. Due diligence, as the name suggests, requires you to be diligent. Being an invested investor is a lot more time-consuming than most people imagine.

Trust your instincts – up to a point. Listen to your gut feelings about an entrepreneur as well as studying the data. Use both in your decision – don't just rely on one or the other.

Start! There's only so much you can learn from other people and the internet, then you have to start learning from your own experience. If you don't write that first cheque, what's the point?

Invest only what you can afford to lose. Your investment pot must include enough for second and possibly third rounds in every investment.

Consider each investment lost once it is made. Although an angel with a large and diverse portfolio may achieve 20% annual return on capital, assuming that investments are lost means that every positive exit is a pleasant surprise.

Invest with other angels. Co-investing not only makes more cash available in the early rounds, it also brings more diverse experiences and skills to support the company.

Be ready to fail. All experienced investors know that some, possibly many, of their companies will fail.

Don't blame others when things go wrong. Each investor makes their own decision to invest – if you end up blaming someone, stop investing.

Be ready to succeed. If you're lucky, you will have one or more stars in your portfolio, and those successes will give you more funds to invest.

Keep going. If at first... and all that.

About the authors

Peter Cowley is a serial entrepreneur and angel investor. He was brought up in Hull and has kept his Yorkshire honesty. He has founded and run a dozen businesses and has invested his own money in more than 65 start-ups. He is the President of the European Business Angel Network and was UK Angel of the Year 2014. He has mentored hundreds of entrepreneurs and is currently on the board of eight start-ups. Peter founded and runs Martlet, the investment arm of the Marshall of Cambridge Group, a privately owned 100-year-old engineering company. He is chair of the Cambridge Angels and is a Fellow in Entrepreneurship at the University of Cambridge Judge Business School. He is a non-executive director of the UK Business Angel Association and on the investment committee of the UK Angel CoFund. He is a popular speaker and travels the world sharing his experiences, good and bad, with entrepreneurs and angel investors.

Kate Kirk is a writer who helps people to tell their stories, covering subjects ranging from the challenges of leading global corporations to what it's like to return to running after a heart attack. She has also written two books about the technology cluster known as 'the Cambridge Phenomenon', and worked with international organisations, world-leading business schools and specialist publishers. For *The Invested Investor*, Kate spent many fascinating hours talking to Peter about the lessons he's learned from decades of entrepreneurship and investing, with the goal of helping him to pass those lessons on in his own, unique way.